HISTORICAL DESSERTS *and* DRINKS
〜 *from the* OFFICERS' KITCHENS *at* FORT YORK 〜

SETTING A FINE TABLE

〜 *Edited by* Elizabeth Baird *and* Bridget Wranich 〜

Research and testing by the Volunteer Historic Cooks at Fort York

whitecap

Whitecap Books

Whitecap Books is known for its expertise in the cookbook market, and has produced some of the most innovative and familiar titles found in kitchens across North America. Visit our website at www.whitecap.ca.

EDITED BY: Theresa Best and Lesley Cameron
DESIGNED BY: Andrew Bagatella
PHOTOGRAPHY: © Pat Crocker/Kate Carlsen (cover, and pages ii, 13, 40, 66, 97, 129); Mark D'Aguilar (page 77); René Malagón (pages 25, 125, 144 [Bridget Wranich]); Marc Rochette (pages 7, 8, 29, 47, 51, 55, 63, 93, 101, 113); Stan Switalski (page 144 [Elizabeth Baird])
FOOD STYLING: Olga Truchan

Printed in Canada

Library and Archives Canada Cataloguing in Publication

Setting a fine table : historical desserts and drinks from the officers' kitchens at Fort York / edited by Elizabeth Baird and Bridget Wranich.

Includes bibliographical references and index.
ISBN 978-1-77050-194-2 (pbk.)

1. Cooking for military personnel—Ontario—Toronto—History—19th century. 2. Great Britain Army—Messes—History—19th century. 3. Desserts—Ontario—Toronto—History—19th century. 4. Beverages—Ontario—Toronto—History—19th century. 5. Fort York (Toronto, Ont.).

I. Baird, Elizabeth, editor of compilation II. Wranich, Bridget, editor of compilation

UC725.C3S48 2013   641.5'7   C2013-904001-3

The publisher acknowledges the financial support of the Government of Canada through the Canada Book Fund (CBF) and the Province of British Columbia through the Book Publishing Tax Credit.

13 14 15 16 17   5 4 3 2 1

CONTENTS

⮌ ACKNOWLEDGEMENTS ⮍

This cookbook is the work of many hands. Over the years many cooks have contributed their research and expertise to the development of the recipes in this book.

We first want to acknowledge all the cooks in the 18th and 19th centuries who worked in the kitchens preparing meals for officers.

Our thanks to Dorothy Duncan who, in the late 1960s, developed a cooking program for the restored historic mess at Fort York.

Thanks to Dr. Carl Benn for his support of the Historic Foodways Programme at Fort York and his recognition that culinary history is a legitimate area of research.

Thanks to Fiona Lucas, who had a huge impact on the growth and development of the Historic Foodways Programme. Her contributions include research and adapting of some of the program's first recipes. Her voice can still be heard in many of the recipes. She also led the way in the development of the Volunteer Historic Cooking Group, which sustains the Historic Foodways Programme.

Thanks to Mya Sangster, the lead cook of the Volunteer Historic Cooking Group. Her dedication to research and her deep understanding of culinary history have had an enormous impact on the success and development of the Historic Foodways Programme.

Thanks also to all the Volunteer Historic Cooks who helped test recipes and support this project: Rosemary Kovac, Ellen Johnstone, John Hammond, Joan Derblich, Kathryn Tanaka, Jan Main, Sherry Murphy, Alexandra Kim, Krystle Forsyth and Emma Vincent.

Thanks to Patrick Gallagher, who encouraged the development of the cookbook and provided excellent advice throughout the project.

Our thanks to Mark D'Aguilar, René Malagón and Marc Rochette for the beautiful images of Fort York. Thanks also to Joy Gordon and Sarah Hood.

We appreciate the generous contribution of food photographer Pat Crocker and her assistants Kate Carlsen and Cindy Brooks, and of food stylist Olga Truchan.

We also appreciate the support of editor Lesley Cameron, the Whitecap Books staff, including editor Theresa Best, art director Michelle Furbacher, designer Andrew Bagatella and especially publisher Nick Rundell, for his enthusiasm for this, our first cookbook project.

Thanks to City of Toronto Museum Services staff who have supported this cookbook project: Karen Black, David O'Hara, Richard Haynes, Kevin Hebib, Kelly Nesbitt, Cheryl Dilisi and Chris Laverton.

∾ INTRODUCTION ∾

Historical recipes are windows into kitchens of the past. They often surprise modern readers, because they are cryptic and lack the structure and instructional tone of our recipes today. I remember when I encountered my first historical recipe—Portugal Cakes from the 1796 edition of Hannah Glasse's *The Art of Cookery Made Plain and Easy.* To my amazement, the recipes in the old cookbook were nothing more elaborate than a collection of titled paragraphs. The visual simplicity was deceptive, though. I read the recipe carefully and realized that making these cakes was going to be challenging. The recipe began, "Mix into a Pound of fine Flour, a Pound of Loaf Sugar beat and sifted . . ." I thought, now what? There wasn't a list of ingredients measured by volume, or a step-by-step method, or an accompanying picture to show me what these cakes should look like. Where could I possibly start? How would I decipher and measure the correct amounts of flour and sugar? The recipe called for ingredients like "rosewater" and "sack"? It wanted me to "plump currants"?

I read the recipe again and tried to imagine combining the flour and sugar, and then rubbing in the butter. This was a very unusual way to make cakes. As I added the rosewater and sack (if you know sack was sherry, this book is definitely for you!) I wondered what rosewater would taste like in the baked cakes, since it certainly wasn't the vanilla extract to which I was accustomed. I noticed the recipe didn't include baking soda or baking powder. How would this cake rise? I painfully discovered that the long time needed to whisk the 10 eggs (both whites and yolks, separately) provided the leavening.

When I eventually finished, I had made a light butter cake batter that was flavoured with currants, rosewater and sherry. I dropped the batter into small, buttered tin pans as the recipe instructed. As I read through the recipe yet again I realized that the only baking instruction was "bake them." How could a recipe not include the temperature? Or the cooking time? I looked at the batter in the tins and decided that they were about the size of modern cupcakes, so I baked them in a 350°F (180°C) oven and estimated the time to be 15 to 20 minutes. The batter was denser than I was accustomed to, so I thought I should keep a close eye on them. My estimation for the time needed turned out to be close. After 18 minutes I took them out of the oven. The cakes had risen to the tops of their pans, and they were a lovely golden brown with currants peeking through. I couldn't wait for them to cool. I removed a cake from its tin and broke it open. The steam rose from it, and the aroma of the sweet rosewater and the yeasty sherry was like nothing I had smelled before. Then I bit into it. I was taken aback by its dense buttery texture and the unfamiliar but delicious flavour. At that very moment I fell in love with historical recipes.

I am part of a group of cooks who have an avid interest in the recipes of the past. Our group participates in an amazing historical cooking program, which connects the past and the present, called the Historic Foodways Programme, at Fort York National Historic Site. As part of the program we research and recreate recipes to illustrate the lifestyle of British officers living in a fort in Upper Canada in the early 19th century. We prepare a wide variety of recipes including soups, roasted and fricasseed meats, fish, salads, vegetable dishes, cakes, pies, tarts, puddings, preserves and pickles.

This cookbook contains a selection of favourite sweet recipes from the Historic Foodways Programme—large and small cakes, pastries, puddings, preserves and drinks—chosen from British, American and Canadian cookbooks from the late 18th and early 19th centuries.

We have three historical kitchens in the Officers' Brick Barracks at Fort York. Two of them are small day kitchens where lighter meals would have been prepared by officers' servants. The third is the 1826 mess kitchen, which is the heart of our program. It best tells the story of the officers stationed at York, and of the operation of a mess establishment that was their exclusive social club and included not only a kitchen, but also a dining room and sitting rooms. The officers regularly entertained notable citizens from the town of York in their mess establishment.

The mess kitchen staff were responsible for preparing the daily main meal shared by the officers in the mess dining room. During the early 19th century, the officers sat down to a formal dinner of two or three courses. The first was savoury, the second a mix of savoury and sweet and the third, the dessert course, a beautifully arranged assortment of sweetmeats, ice creams, jellies and more (see photo page 101).

The mess sergeant, or mess man, who was responsible for overseeing the entire operation of the mess, composed the menu for the officers. His role was comparable to that of a butler in a household. He not only set the menus, but also hired the cooks, ordered the supplies, kept the accounts and issued the officers' monthly mess bills.

The cooks were most often women, either soldiers' wives or civilians from the town. Research has revealed only a little about these women. The first cook we can identify is Mary Casey, listed as a cook on an army pay list. In 1813, she signed for her pay with an X. Another cook, Mrs. Chapman, is mentioned in the diary of Eli Playter, a local militia officer. This dedicated servant was found working in the fort during the Battle of York in 1813 and was told to leave immediately for her own safety. On the same day, another female servant was found hiding in a potato locker in the lieutenant governor's house.

As modern cooks, those of us who belong to the Historic Food-ways Programme have the opportunity to step back into the roles of the women who stirred the pots, roasted the meats and filled the bake oven two centuries ago. We do this by becoming recipe archaeologists. We treat the recipes from the past as artifacts. As archaeologists, we dig through recipes from cookbooks of that period, collecting, compar-ing and analyzing them. We then use these tried and true recipes, both sweet and savoury, for demonstrations in Fort York's historical kitchens, cooking classes and special events, such as the annual commemoration of the Battle of York. The best test of our recipes is when we set menus for large-scale events such as our Georgian Mess Dinner and Queen Charlotte's Birthday Ball.

We are always respectful of the original intent of the cookbook writer. We make the recipes over and over again, refining ingredients, methods and equipment, keeping the results as close as possible to how we think the original would have been. We stock our shelves with period ingredients like rosewater, orange flower water, sack (sherry), brandy, port, white wine vinegar, bitter almonds, whole nutmegs, long pepper, bay leaves, whole turmeric and ginger, cardamom pods, coriander and cumin seeds, candied angelica and citrus peel, and an abundance of currants and caraway seeds. Butter varied in quality, sugar came in cone-shaped loaves and eggs were smaller, more like our medium-size eggs. While we need to compensate for these differences, balancing traditional flavours and methods, our goal is to share the authentic tastes.

Visitors to the 1826 kitchen love to see beautifully raised cakes, fragrant with spices, coming out of the bake oven, puddings boiling over the fire and meats roasting over the coals. They are intrigued by our hoops (metal hoops lined with paper) for baking cakes, pudding cloths, cutters, and mortar and pestles, and often exclaim how they bring back memories of their grandmother's kitchen—it seems that in some places the equipment and techniques have not changed much over the years. This is true of visitors not only from North America but also from homelands as diverse as Poland, China and India.

This cookbook celebrates these historical recipes. We've opted to include only sweet recipes because those are the ones most frequently requested by our visitors. Each recipe includes the text of the original recipe, with the name of the cookbook in which we found it, some interesting historical notes and a modern equivalent for making the recipe at home. The cookbook is a way for us to preserve and share traditional tastes and provides an opportunity for you—whether you are a first-, second- or third-generation Canadian, or descended from the early settlers or First Nations—to connect with our past and our country's past through these recipes.

—Bridget Wranich,
Program Officer,
Fort York National Historic Site

The 1826 kitchen, the heart of Fort York's Historic Foodways Programme,
is called the mess kitchen.

THE RECIPES

Shrewsbury Cakes

BEAT half a pound of butter to a fine cream, and put in the same weight of flour, one egg, six ounces of beaten and sifted loaf sugar, and half an ounce of carraway seeds. Mix them into a paste, roll them thin, and cut them round with a small glass or little tins; prick them, lay them on sheets of tin, and bake them in a slow oven.

HISTORIC RECIPE EXCERPTED FROM
The London Art of Cookery
(John Farley, 1800)

~ SHREWSBURY CAKES ~

Shrewsbury cakes are one of the most popular recipes that we make at Fort York. For many of the visitors who sample these crisp, buttery "cakes" (cookies) in the historical kitchen, the caraway seeds in the recipe are first a novelty, then a delightful surprise. The original recipe uses less flour and is difficult to roll out. Our modern equivalent includes more flour, is easier to roll out and still makes a delicious crisp cookie.

HISTORICAL BACKGROUND

Shrewsbury Cakes are a regional cake from the county town of Shrewsbury (pronounced *SHROES*-burr-ee) in Shropshire, England. They are sometimes also referred to as Shropshire cakes. Shrewsbury cakes were rolled out, cut into shapes, pricked (using a pin or comb), flavoured with caraway seeds or spices and, in some recipes, perfumed with rosewater or brandy and/or sprinkled with sugar.

Caraway was introduced to Britain by the Romans and was popular in biscuits and cakes. There are references to caraway in cookery books from as early as the 16th century, but it had fallen out of favour by the late 20th century, although it continued to be used in some breads. The cultivation of caraway started in Upper Canada in the early 19th century.

1 cup (250 mL) unsalted butter, softened

1 cup (250 mL) granulated sugar

4 tsp (20 mL) caraway seeds

1 medium egg

2¼ cups (560 mL) all-purpose flour

Line 2 rimless baking sheets with parchment paper, or lightly grease.

In a large bowl, beat the butter and sugar until light and fluffy. Beat in the caraway seeds, then the egg. Stir in the flour in 3 batches.

Press the dough together, kneading gently until smooth. Divide in half and shape into 2 discs.

(Make-ahead: Wrap each disc of dough separately and refrigerate for up to 1 day. Bring to room temperature to soften before rolling.)

Roll out the dough, one disc at a time, on a well-floured work surface to a ¼-inch (5 mm) thickness. Using a fluted 2-inch (5 cm) cookie cutter, cut the dough into rounds. Arrange the cookies 1 inch (2.5 cm) apart on the prepared baking sheets. Using a comb and small skewer, press a diamond and dot pattern on each cake. Form the scraps into a disc and reroll for more cookies.

Bake in the centre of a 350°F (180°C) oven until light golden on the bottom, about 12 to 15 minutes. Let firm up on the baking sheets for 3 minutes, then transfer to racks to cool completely.

(Make-ahead: Layer in airtight containers. Store at room temperature for a few days or freeze, for up to 2 weeks.)

Makes about 70 cookies.

Hard Gingerbread

ONE pound of butter, one of sugar, one pint of molasses, one teacup of ginger, three teaspoons of pearlash, flour enough to make a stiff dough, spice to your taste.

HISTORIC RECIPE EXCERPTED FROM
The Cook Not Mad; Or, Rational Cookery
(Anonymous, 1831)

~ HARD GINGERBREAD ~

*When Fort York cooks worked on a modern
version of this recipe, they first tried it out, as directed, with a teacup
(about ¾ cup/185 mL) of ground ginger, and then added a variety of other
spices that were historically accurate—cinnamon, nutmeg, Jamaica
pepper (allspice), mace, cloves, anise, caraway and black pepper. The
gingerbread was snappy indeed! The blend of spices in the modern version
below, which has been sampled by thousands of Fort York visitors, has less
ginger and is a real crowd-pleaser. You can cut the dough into all kinds of
shapes, depending on the season and holiday. At the Fort,
soldier shapes are popular.*

HISTORICAL BACKGROUND

Early gingerbreads were unbaked confections made of breadcrumbs, honey and spices. Through the Middle Ages they were shaped and gilded and then displayed as decorative centrepieces on banquet tables. In the early 17th century, gingerbread transitioned into a baked biscuit (cookie) when almonds and flour replaced the breadcrumbs and treacle (molasses) replaced the honey. The dough was pressed into moulds or stamped with cutters into shapes such as animals, flowers, birds or men. Some villages in England had a tradition whereby unmarried women had to eat gingerbread "husbands" if they wanted to meet a real husband. By the 18th century, gingerbread biscuits were being sold by vendors at country fairs and were a very popular street food. According to military records, British officers occasionally gave regular soldiers gingerbread with their rations on special occasions such as the King's birthday.

HARD GINGERBREAD (CONT'D)

OUR MODERN EQUIVALENT

·◁————╌◈╌————▷·

1 cup (250 mL) unsalted butter, softened

1 cup (250 mL) granulated sugar

1 cup (250 mL) fancy molasses

4 cups (1 L) all-purpose flour

2 Tbsp (30 mL) ground ginger

1 tsp (5 mL) ground allspice

1 tsp (5 mL) ground cinnamon

1 tsp (5 mL) grated nutmeg

1 tsp (5 mL) baking soda

Line 2 rimless baking sheets with parchment paper, or lightly grease.

In a large bowl, beat the butter and sugar until light and fluffy. Beat in the molasses until smooth.

In a separate large bowl, whisk together the flour, ginger, allspice, cinnamon, nutmeg and baking soda. Stir into the molasses mixture 1 cup (250 mL) at a time. Press the dough together, kneading gently a few times until smooth. Divide in half.

(Make-ahead: Form each half of the dough into a disc, wrap separately and chill until firm, about 1 hour. Let soften slightly at room temperature before rolling.)

Roll out the dough, one disc at a time, on a well-floured work surface to ⅛-inch (3 mm) thickness. Using plain or fancy cookie cutters, cut into shapes. Arrange 1 inch (2.5 cm) apart on the prepared baking sheets. Form the scraps into a disc and reroll for more cookies.

Bake in the centre of a 350°F (180°C) oven until slightly darkened on the bottom and firm to a light touch, about 10 to 12 minutes. Let firm up on the baking sheets for 3 minutes, then transfer to racks to cool completely.

(Make-ahead: Layer in airtight containers. Store at room temperature for a few days or freeze for up to 2 weeks.)

Makes about ninety 2-inch (5 cm) cookies.

❁   ❁   ❁   ❁

TIP The historic recipe makes double the amount of dough than this recipe does, and is ideal for larger gingerbread projects, such as a gingerbread house or Christmas tree decorations, or for throwing a gingerbread cookie party. For a larger amount of dough, simply double the amounts of all the ingredients in our modern equivalent.

TIP Pearlash (potassium carbonate), the traditional leavening ingredient, is often available in German delicatessens. To use, omit the baking soda and dissolve 2 tsp (10 mL) pearlash in 2 tsp (10 mL) milk. Add to the batter with the molasses.

Orange Gingerbread

Two pounds and a quarter fine flour, a pound and three quarters molasses, twelve ounces of sugar, three ounces undried orange peel chopped fine, one ounce each of ginger and allspice, melt twelve ounces of butter, mix the whole together, lay it by for twelve hours, roll it out with as little flour as possible, cut it in pieces three inches wide, mark them in the form of checkers with the back of a knife, rub them over with the yelk of an egg, beat with a teacup of milk, when done wash them again with the egg.

HISTORIC RECIPE EXCERPTED FROM
The Cook Not Mad; Or, Rational Cookery
(Anonymous, 1831)

~ ORANGE GINGERBREAD ~

*For the "undried orange peel chopped fine" called for in the
original recipe, there are two options: finely diced candied orange peel,
which culinary historians feel is more authentic, or finely grated
fresh orange peel, for more assertive citrus accents.*

HISTORICAL BACKGROUND

The British were importing bitter and sweet oranges from Portugal in
the late 16th century. No part of the orange was wasted. Preserving the
flavour of orange peel by candying and drying it became popular in the
early 17th century. To candy orange peel at that time, cooks boiled and
reboiled the orange peel in sugar syrup, sometimes over several days.
This was an excellent way to keep the delicious citrus flavour for baking cakes, biscuits and puddings. Bitter oranges such as Sevilles made a
more intensely flavoured candied peel.

A year before *The Cook Not Mad* was published in Upper Canada, Dr. William Kitchener's American edition of *The Cook's Oracle*
included this same recipe—even down to the scoring. In this era, recipes were often copied from one cookbook to another without credit.

·⊂━━━━━⊃·

DOUGH

¾ cup (185 mL) unsalted butter

1½ cups (375 mL) fancy molasses

¼ cup (60 mL) very finely diced candied orange peel or
grated orange rind (zest)

4 cups (1 L) all-purpose flour

¾ cup (185 mL) granulated sugar

1 Tbsp (15 mL) ground ginger

1 Tbsp (15 mL) ground allspice

GLAZE

1 medium egg yolk

¼ cup (60 mL) milk

Line 2 rimless baking sheets with parchment paper, or lightly grease.

For the dough, in a saucepan over medium heat, melt the butter and molasses just until smooth. Scrape into a large bowl and let cool to room temperature. Add the candied orange peel.

In a separate large bowl, whisk together the flour, sugar, ginger and allspice. Stir into the molasses mixture 1 cup (250 mL) at a time. Press the dough together, kneading a few times until smooth. Divide in half and form each half into a disc.

(Make-ahead: Wrap each disc individually and chill until firm, about 1 hour or up to overnight. Let soften at room temperature before rolling.)

Roll out each disc on a well-floured work surface to a 15- × 9-inch (38 × 23 cm) rectangle, a scant ¼ inch (6 mm) thick. Trim if necessary. With the blunt side of a long knife or ruler, press lines about halfway through the dough, 1 inch (2.5 cm) apart, first vertically, then horizontally, to form a neat checkerboard pattern. Cut into 3-inch (8 cm) squares and transfer to the prepared baking sheets, about 1 inch (2.5 cm) apart.

For the glaze, in a small bowl, beat the egg yolk with the milk until smooth. Brush about half of the mixture over the gingerbread squares.

Bake in the centre of a 350°F (180°C) oven until firm to a light touch and darkened on the bottom, about 15 to 18 minutes. Immediately brush with the remaining glaze mixture. Let firm up on the baking sheets for 3 minutes, then transfer to racks to cool completely.

(Make-ahead: Layer the squares in airtight containers. Store at room temperature for a few days or freeze for up to 2 weeks.)

Makes about 50 squares.

Jumbles

HALF a pound of butter, half a pound of sugar, three quarters of a pound of flour, two eggs, rolled in sugar and nutmeg; to be dropped on tins to bake.

HISTORIC RECIPE EXCERPTED FROM

The Cook Not Mad; Or, Rational Cookery

(Anonymous, 1831)

~ JUMBLES ~

*Throughout the year, Fort York buzzes with schoolchildren
experiencing Canadian history first hand. There are drills, crafts and
lessons, and for part of the day the students gather in the officers'
mess kitchen to make jumbles, a recipe with plenty of steps, making it ideal
for groups of young cooks who can each play a part. Some grate nutmeg,
while others pound the sugar, beat the butter, blend in the flour or break
eggs. Once the buttery dough is pressed together, everyone shapes it into
balls and rolls them in a sugar/nutmeg combo. The children enjoy this
delicious treat before boarding their buses to go home.*

HISTORICAL BACKGROUND

Recipes for jumbles first appeared in medieval cookery books. One of
the earliest recipes we have found is from Gervais Markham's *The English
Housewife* (1615).

The word "jumble" is derived from the Latin "geminus" meaning
"twin." They were also referred to in early recipes as "jumbals," "jumbolds," "jamballs," "jemelloes," "gumballs" or "gemballs." Shape rather
than flavour characterized early jumbles. Originally, thin ropes of the
dough were twisted into pretzel shapes, figure eights, circlets or symmetrical knots. Some jumbles were fruit pastes rather than flour-based
biscuits (cookies). By the late 18th century, the word was being used to
describe biscuits (cookies) that were rolled flat and stamped with circular cutters. *The Cook Not Mad* contains four different jumbles recipes:

one with caraway seeds rolled in sugar, one that instructs the baker to "use any good spice you like," one called Jackson Jumbles (raised with pearlash) and the Fort's favourite, called simply Jumbles, rolled in sugar and freshly grated nutmeg.

OUR MODERN EQUIVALENT

DOUGH

1 cup (250 mL) unsalted butter, softened

1 cup (250 mL) granulated sugar

2 medium eggs

3 cups (750 mL) all-purpose flour

ROLLING MIXTURE

¼ cup (60 mL) granulated sugar

2 tsp (10 mL) grated nutmeg

Line 2 rimless baking sheets with parchment paper, or lightly grease.

For the dough, in a large bowl, beat the butter and sugar until light and fluffy. Beat in the eggs, one at a time. Stir in the flour, 1 cup (250 mL) at a time, to make a smooth dough. Set aside.

For the rolling mixture, in a shallow bowl, stir together the sugar and nutmeg.

Scoop the dough by well-rounded teaspoons (7 mL) and roll into balls ¾ inch (2 cm) in diameter. Roll the balls, one at a time, in the nutmeg mixture, pressing gently to coat the surface. Place them about 1 inch (2.5 cm) apart on the prepared baking sheets.

Bake in the centre of a 350°F (180°C) oven until golden on the bottom, about 15 minutes. Let firm up on baking sheets for 3 minutes, then transfer to racks to cool completely.

(Make-ahead: Layer the balls in airtight containers. Store at room temperature for a few days or freeze for up to 2 weeks.)

Makes about 56 jumbles.

❀   ❀   ❀   ❀

TIP In the historical kitchen, young cooks grate fresh nutmeg using a small pierced metal grater available in cookware shops. Look for whole nutmegs in some supermarkets, West Indian shops and specialty stores.

Mackeroons

Take a pound of almonds, let them be scalded, blanched, and thrown into cold water, then dry them in a cloth, and pound them in a mortar, moisten them with orange-flower water, or with the white of an egg, lest they turn to oil; afterwards, take an equal quantity of fine powder sugar, with three or four whites of eggs, and a little musk, beat all well together, and shape them on wafer-paper, with a spoon round: bake them in a gentle oven on tin plates.

HISTORIC RECIPE EXCERPTED FROM
The Art of Cookery Made Plain and Easy
(Hannah Glasse, 1796)

~ MACKEROONS ~

*These almond mackeroons are a go-to recipe when we are baking
samples to offer to visitors in the 1826 kitchen. Our volunteer historical
cooks separate the egg whites into a big copper bowl and, with a whisk,
hand-beat the egg whites to glossy peaks or, as some 18th-century recipes say,
"to a stiff froth." At home, a stand or hand mixer makes light work of the
whisking. Either method produces handsome mackeroons.*

HISTORICAL BACKGROUND

Today, mackeroons (now spelled *macaroons*) are a meringue made with
coconut, but until the mid-19th century they contained finely chopped
or pounded sweet almonds. Recipes for mackeroons appeared frequently in 17th- and 18th-century cookery books, with varying ratios
of sugar to egg whites. Mackeroons were served with wines and liqueurs,
or were crushed and layered in trifles or with syllabubs and creams.

Orange blossom water and rosewater, both made by steeping the
flower blossoms in brandy or distilled water, were characteristic flavourings for this biscuit (cookie). Musk, another popular flavouring, is
an aromatic substance produced by the male musk-deer. It is still an
important ingredient in perfumery, but is no longer considered edible.
By the mid-19th century, vanilla had displaced these flavourings.

MACKEROONS (CONT'D)

OUR MODERN EQUIVALENT

3 cups (750 mL) whole blanched almonds

4 medium egg whites (½ cup/125 mL)

2 tsp (10 mL) orange flower water

2 cups (500 mL) superfine granulated sugar

Line 2 rimless baking sheets with parchment paper.

In a food processor, chop the almonds, scraping down the sides of the bowl from time to time, until they are the consistency of very coarse sand with some slightly larger pieces. Set aside.

In a separate large bowl, beat the egg whites with the orange flower water until soft peaks form. Add the sugar about 2 Tbsp (30 mL) at a time, beating until stiff peaks form. Sprinkle the chopped almonds over the egg white mixture and fold in to distribute evenly.

Drop by rounded teaspoonfuls (6 mL) about 1 inch (2.5 cm) apart onto the prepared baking sheets. Bake in the centre of a 325°F (160°C) oven until they are dry to the touch, but still white, and lift easily off the parchment paper, about 12 to 15 minutes.

Let cool on the pans on a rack.

(Make-ahead: Layer in airtight containers. Store at room temperature for a few days or freeze for up to 2 weeks.)

Makes about 80 mackeroons.

Peppermint Drops

Pound and sift four ounces of doubly refined sugar, beat it with whites of two eggs till perfectly smooth; then add sixty drops of oil of peppermint, beat it well, and drop on white paper, and dry at a distance from the fire.

HISTORIC RECIPE EXCERPTED FROM

A New System of Domestic Cookery,
Formed Upon the Principles of Economy

(Maria Eliza Rundell, 1806)

~ PEPPERMINT DROPS ~

Low heat in the oven is all that's needed to dry these drops—
the 18th-century equivalent of after-dinner mints. You can buy superfine
sugar or make it by whirling regular granulated sugar in a food processor
until the granules are half their original size.

HISTORICAL BACKGROUND

The "oil of peppermint" that Mrs. Rundell used may have been purchased from her local apothecary, who would have made it by extracting the essential oil from the leaves and flowers of fresh peppermint. Alternatively, she may have made it herself by repeatedly steeping fresh peppermint leaves in light olive oil. Sixty drops equals a standard teaspoon.

OUR MODERN EQUIVALENT

2 medium egg whites

¾ cup (185 mL) superfine granulated sugar

10 drops peppermint oil or 1 tsp (5 mL) peppermint extract

Red or green food colouring (optional)

Line 2 rimless baking sheets with parchment paper.

In a medium bowl, beat the egg whites until soft peaks form. Beat in the sugar 2 Tbsp (30 mL) at a time until glossy firm peaks form when the beaters are raised. Fold in the peppermint oil. If desired, divide the meringue into 3 separate bowls, adding 1 to 2 drops of green food colouring into one of the bowls, slightly less of the red food colouring into the second bowl and leaving the third bowl of meringue white.

Drop the meringue mixture by ½ tsp (2 mL) onto the prepared pans, leaving 1 inch (2.5 cm) between mounds. Or scoop the mixture into a piping bag fitted with a star tip and pipe out small rosettes. Each mound of batter should be the size of a nickel.

Place in a 150°F (65°C) oven until dry to the touch, about 30 to 40 minutes. Watch carefully and turn off the oven if the drops start to brown. Leave in the oven and let cool completely.

(Make-ahead: Layer in airtight containers. Store at room temperature for up to 3 weeks.)

Makes about 60 peppermint drops.

❀   ❀   ❀   ❀

TIP Look for peppermint oil in cake decorating shops or bulk food stores. Make sure the peppermint oil is food grade. Peppermint extract can be substituted, but more will be needed to equal the more intense flavour of the peppermint oil.

ART
OF
COOKERY.

Frontispiece from Maria Eliza Rundell's
A New System of Domestic Cookery (1806)

Lemon Puffs

TAKE a pound and a quarter of double-refin'd Sugar beaten and sifted, and grate the Rinds of two Lemons, and mix well with the Sugar; then beat the whites of three new-laid Eggs very well, and mix it well with your Sugar and Lemon-peel; beat them together an hour and a quarter, then make it up in what form you please; be quick to set them in a moderate Oven; don't take them off the Papers till cold.

HISTORIC RECIPE EXCERPTED FROM
The Compleat Housewife
(Eliza Smith, 1727)

～ LEMON PUFFS ～

Cake recipes from the Fort's era often used more egg yolks than egg whites and, like the cooks of the 18th and early 19th centuries, the staff and volunteer historical cooks at the Fort are always keen to find ways to use the leftover whites. These lemon puffs, tangy, sweet and melt-in-your-mouth, are an ideal option, as are Mackeroons (page 27) and Peppermint Drops (page 31).

HISTORICAL BACKGROUND

Lemon puffs are actually a meringue. Meringue (beaten egg whites and sugar) was first introduced to British cooks by the English translation of Massialot's *Court and Country Cook*, in 1702. Sometimes, puffs were flavoured with almonds, caraway seeds and even chocolate. They were often purchased from confectionery shops rather than made at home.

Puffs were part of a dessert course, the third course of a Georgian dinner, along with other sweetmeats, such as Peppermint Drops (page 31), Mackeroons (page 27) and fruit pastes. (See page 101 for a photograph of a dessert course with nuts, fruit and cheese displayed on the dining table in the officers' mess at Fort York National Historic Site.)

·◁———※———▷·

3 cups (750 mL) granulated sugar
2 Tbsp (30 mL) finely grated lemon rind (zest)
3 medium egg whites

Line 2 rimless baking sheets with parchment paper.

In a medium bowl, whisk together the sugar and lemon rind.

In a large bowl, beat the egg whites until soft peaks form. Adding the sugar mixture 2 Tbsp (30 mL) at a time, beat at high speed until thick and the beaters leave ridges in the meringue mixture.

Drop by rounded teaspoons (6 mL) onto the prepared pans, leaving about 1 inch (2.5 cm) between mounds.

Bake in the centre of a 250°F (120°C) oven until firm but not browned, 10 to 15 minutes. The puffs should lift easily off the parchment paper. Let cool on the pan on a rack.

(Make-ahead: Layer in airtight containers. Store at room temperature for up to 2 weeks.)

Makes about 70 lemon puffs.

The COMPLEAT HOUSEWIFE. *frontispiece*

Printed for R.Ware,T.Longman, S.Birt, C.Hitch,J.Hodges.
J.&J.Rivington, J.Ward,W.Johnston,& M.Cooper.

THE

Compleat Housewife:

OR,

Accomplish'd Gentlewoman's

COMPANION.

BEING

A COLLECTION of upwards of Six Hundred
of the most approved RECEIPTS in

COOKERY,	CAKES,
PASTRY,	CREAMS,
CONFECTIONARY,	JELLIES,
PRESERVING,	MADE WINES,
PICKLES,	CORDIALS.

With COPPER PLATES curiously engraven for
the regular Disposition or Placing the various
DISHES and COURSES.

AND ALSO

BILLS of FARE for every Month in the Year.
To which is added,

A COLLECTION of above Three Hundred Family RECEIPTS
of MEDICINES; viz. Drinks, Syrups, Salves, Ointments,
and various other Things of sovereign and approved Efficacy
in most Distempers, Pains, Aches, Wounds, Sores, &c.
particularly Mrs. Stephens's Medicine for the Cure of the Stone
and Gravel, and Dr. Mead's famous Receipt for the Cure of a
Bite of a mad Dog; with several other excellent Receipts for
the same, which have cured when the Persons were disordered,
and the salt Water fail'd; never before made publick; fit
either for private Families, or such publick-spirited Gentle-
women as would be beneficent to their poor Neighbours.

By E. SMITH.

The FOURTEENTH EDITION,
To which is now first prefixed,

DIRECTIONS for MARKETING.

LONDON:
Printed for R. Ware, S. Birt, T. Longman, C. Hitch, J. Hodges,
J. and J. Rivington, J. Ward, W. Johnston, and M. Cooper.
M. DCC, L.

Price FIVE SHILLINGS.

Frontispiece and title page from Eliza Smith's *The Compleat Housewife* (1727)

A Seed Cake, Very Rich

Take a Pound of Flour dried, a Pound of Sugar beaten and sifted, a Pound of Butter work'd with your Hand to a Cream: Beat the yolks of ten Eggs, six Whites, and mix all together; an Ounce of Carraway Seeds, and a Gill of Brandy. Keep it beating till you put it in the Oven.

HISTORIC RECIPE EXCERPTED FROM
A New and Easy Method of Cookery
(Elizabeth Cleland, 1755)

~ A SEED CAKE, VERY RICH ~

*The historical kitchen at the Fort goes through an astonishing
quantity of caraway seeds, the seed that gives this popular pound cake
its distinctive, appealing and, to many visitors, unfamiliar, even elusive
flavour. What's noteworthy about this cake, aside from its deliciousness
and moist, dense texture, is cookbook author Elizabeth Cleland's
instruction to work the butter to a cream with your hand. This is indeed
what staff and volunteers do when showcasing this recipe in the historical
kitchen, but beating the butter with a mixer also produces a very fine cake.
A "gill" of brandy is ½ cup (125 mL).*

HISTORICAL BACKGROUND

This cake is a true pound cake as it calls for 1 pound each of flour, sugar and butter. Pound cakes were often flavoured with caraway seeds as well as lemon, brandy or currants. Early seed cakes were raised by the addition of yeast. Initially, eggs were added to enrich the cakes and, as recipes evolved, they eventually replaced the yeast as leavening. In the 18th century, it was popular to serve seed cakes at harvest time. These pound cakes were dense and moist with a fine crumb, quite unlike the light, airy, commercial pound cakes of today.

At that time cooks baked a variety of cakes—for example, plum cakes, like our modern fruit cake—for special occasions such as weddings or funerals. Some of these cakes were very large, calling for a peck (around 36 cups/9 L) of flour, 3 pounds of currants and up to a dozen eggs. The cakes were baked in wide wooden hoops wrapped in paper and set on metal sheets to bake.

·⊂═══╳═══⊃·

2 cups (500 mL) butter, softened

2 cups (500 mL) superfine granulated sugar

6 medium eggs, separated

4 medium egg yolks

3½ cups (875 mL) all-purpose flour

¼ cup (60 mL) caraway seeds

½ cup (125 mL) brandy

Line the sides and bottom of a 10-inch (3.5 L) springform pan with 3 layers of parchment paper.

In a large bowl, beat the butter until very fluffy and cream coloured. Beat in the sugar 2 Tbsp (30 mL) at a time. Beat in the 10 egg yolks, one at a time, beating well after each addition. Place the 6 egg whites in a large, clean bowl and set aside.

In a separate bowl, whisk together the flour and caraway seeds. Stir into the butter mixture in 3 additions, alternating with the brandy in 2 additions.

Beat the reserved egg whites to stiff but not dry peaks. Stir about one-third of the whites into the batter, then fold in the remainder to make a smooth, even batter.

Scrape into the prepared pan, smooth the top and tap the pan lightly on the work surface to eliminate any air bubbles.

Bake in the centre of a 325°F (160°C) oven until the cake has come away from the side of the pan and a toothpick inserted into the centre comes out clean, about 3 hours. This sounds like a long time, but the cake is very dense. To ensure doneness, insert an instant-read thermometer into the centre of the cake. The interior temperature should be 205°F (96°C). Let cool in the pan on a rack for 20 minutes, then turn out onto the rack to cool completely.

(Make-ahead: Wrap well in foil and store in an airtight container at room temperature for up to a few days, or wrap in heavy-duty foil and freeze for up to 2 weeks.)

To serve, cut crosswise into generous ½-inch (1 cm) wide slices, not wedges. Then cut the slices into pieces or fingers.

Makes about 70 pieces.

❀　❀　❀　❀

TIP To make a smaller seed cake, halve the ingredients. Follow the method above, but bake the cake in an 8-inch (2 L) springform pan in the centre of a 325°F (160°C) oven for about 2 hours.

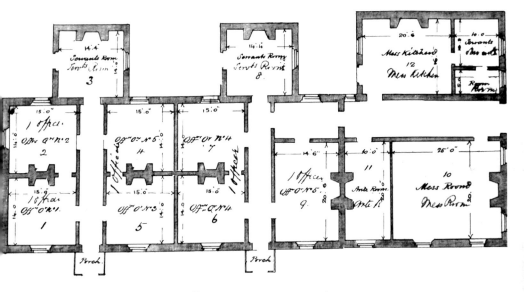

-.GROUND.PLAN.-

Height of rooms 10 feet.

Floor plan (1865) showing the mess kitchen and mess sergeant's quarters
(top right). In 1826, these were added to the 1815 Officers' Brick Barracks and
mess dining room (bottom right).

Soft Gingerbread with Fruit

ONE pound and a half of flour, half a pound of sugar, half a pound of butter, one pint of molasses, four eggs, one tea cup of milk, two teaspoons of pearlash, one ounce of ginger, one of cinnamon, one nutmeg, one pound of currants.

HISTORIC RECIPE EXCERPTED FROM

The Cook Not Mad; Or, Rational Cookery

(Anonymous, 1831)

～ SOFT GINGERBREAD WITH FRUIT ～

At Fort York, this dense and deliciously spicy cake
is baked in a traditional wood-burning bake oven, or on a down-hearth
in a large oval copper braising kettle set over coals from the fire, with more
coals added to the kettle's rimmed and inverted cover (see photo page 47).
The heat from top and bottom bakes the cake evenly in about the same time
as it takes to bake this cake in a modern oven. The original recipe has been
halved to fit contemporary pans and appetites.

HISTORICAL BACKGROUND

This recipe for soft gingerbread follows an innovation of the late 18th century, in which milk and eggs were added to traditional European hard gingerbread dough (see Hard Gingerbread on page 15) to make a softer biscuit (cookie) or cake.

Prior to the invention of chemical leavening agents such as pearlash, and later baking soda, it was common to need at least eight eggs for leavening for the most basic cake. *The Cook Not Mad* is one of the earliest books to include recipes that use chemicals as a supplement to eggs, and fewer eggs are required for leavening this cake. The author writes, "Let it be observed and understood that all cake is better to beat yelks and whites of eggs separately, and adding the whites just before going into the oven."

OUR MODERN EQUIVALENT

2 cups (500 mL) currants

½ cup (125 mL) butter, softened

¾ cup (185 mL) granulated sugar

2 medium eggs, separated

1 cup (250 mL) fancy molasses

2¾ cups (685 mL) all-purpose flour

3½ Tbsp (50 mL) ground ginger

2½ Tbsp (37 mL) ground cinnamon

2½ tsp (12 mL) grated nutmeg

1 tsp (5 mL) baking soda

½ cup (125 mL) whole milk

Line the bottom and sides of a 10-inch (3 L) springform pan with parchment paper. Butter the parchment paper on the bottom of the pan.

Soak the currants in hot water for 5 minutes. Drain and spread out to dry on a towel-lined tray, about 15 minutes.

Meanwhile, in a large bowl, beat the butter and sugar until very light and fluffy.

In a separate bowl, beat the egg yolks until thick and light-coloured, about 5 minutes. Stir into the butter mixture, followed by the molasses. Set aside the egg whites.

In another bowl, whisk together the flour, ginger, cinnamon, nutmeg and baking soda. Stir into the butter mixture in 3 additions, alternating with the milk in 2 additions. Sprinkle the currants over the batter.

In a clean bowl, beat the 2 reserved egg whites until stiff, glossy, moist peaks form. Stir about one-third of the beaten whites into the batter with the currants. Fold in the remaining egg whites.

Scrape the batter into the prepared pan, tapping the pan gently on the work surface to eliminate any air bubbles. Smooth the top.

Bake in the centre of a 350°F (180°C) oven until the cake comes away from the edges, the perfume of spices is overwhelming and a toothpick inserted into the middle comes out clean, about 1½ hours.

Let cool in the pan on a rack for 20 minutes. Loosen the side of the pan and slide the cake onto a rack to finish cooling.

(Make-ahead: Wrap and store at room temperature for up to a few days, or wrap in heavy-duty foil and freeze for up to 2 weeks.)

Makes 1 large cake, about 30 pieces.

Copper braising kettle
(see the introduction to the recipe, page 45)

Little Fine Cakes

ONE Pound of Butter beat to Cream, a Pound and a quarter of Flour, a Pound of fine Sugar beat fine, a Pound of Currants clean wash'd and pick'd, six Eggs, two Whites left out, beat them fine, mix the Flour, Sugar, and Eggs by Degrees into the Butter, beat it all well with both Hands; either make into little Cakes, or bake it in one.

HISTORIC RECIPE EXCERPTED FROM
The Art of Cookery Made Plain and Easy
(Hannah Glasse, 1796)

~ LITTLE FINE CAKES ~

*In the mid-19th century, bakers counted on eggs to provide
the rising power. Even with a generous number of eggs, these Little Fine
Cakes are dense—the texture is closer to that of a rich, buttery pound cake
than today's airy cupcakes. Enjoy with tea or coffee, or a glass of port. In the
early days, guests of the officers enjoyed wine and cakes—
perhaps one like this.*

HISTORICAL BACKGROUND

Currants were a popular dried fruit for flavouring cakes. They did not
need stoning like raisins, and only needed to be washed, plumped and
picked to remove any stems. Plumping involved pouring hot, or even
boiling, water over them and letting them soak by the fire. The currants
were then drained and returned to the hearth to dry.

This recipe calls for "two whites left out"; that is, it uses more yolks
than whites. According to culinary historian Karen Hess in her book,
Martha Washington's Booke of Cookery, this popular practice was followed because cooks understood the effects of egg yolks and whites
in batters. They believed the yolks added richness and created a deli-
cate texture. The whites were added to strengthen the batter, but cooks
feared that too many could toughen the texture.

·⟨━━━━━⟩·

2½ cups (625 mL) currants

2 cups (500 mL) unsalted butter, softened

2 cups (500 mL) granulated sugar

4 medium eggs

2 medium egg yolks

4 cups (1 L) all-purpose flour

Grease 24 muffin cups. Line the bottom of each with parchment paper cut to fit.

Soak the currants in hot water for 5 minutes. Drain and spread out to dry on a towel-lined tray, about 15 minutes.

Meanwhile, in a large bowl, beat the butter until very fluffy and cream coloured. Beat in the sugar ½ cup (125 mL) at a time.

In a separate bowl, beat the eggs and yolks until very thick, light coloured and glossy, about 10 minutes. Beat them into the butter mixture in 2 additions.

Stir the currants, then the flour, 1 cup (250 mL) at a time, into the butter mixture. Spoon into the prepared muffin cups.

Bake in the centre of a 350°F (180°C) oven until the cakes are golden brown and firm on top and a toothpick inserted into the centre comes out clean, 20 to 25 minutes. Let cool in the pans on a rack for 10 minutes. Loosen the cakes with a blunt knife and turn them onto the rack to cool completely.

(Make-ahead: Layer in an airtight container and store at room temperature for up to a few days, or freeze for up to 2 weeks.)

Makes about 24 small cakes.

❀ ❀ ❀ ❀

TIP For a dozen Little Fine Cakes, simply halve the ingredients.

Heart Cakes

Work one pound of butter to a cream with the hand, put to it twelve yolks of eggs and six whites, well beaten, one pound of sifted sugar, one pound of flour dried, four spoonfuls of the best brandy, one pound of currants washed and dried before the fire; as the pans are filled put in two ounces of candied orange and citron; beat the cakes till they go into the oven: this quantity will fill three dozen of middling pans.

HISTORIC RECIPE EXCERPTED FROM
The Lady's Assistant
(Charlotte Mason, 1787)

~ HEART CAKES ~

Although part of the appeal of these fruity little cakes is their shape, you can bake them in a regular muffin pan. However, pans with heart-shaped cups are readily available in cookware shops, and can also be used to make modern small cakes such as cupcakes, brownies or muffins.

HISTORICAL BACKGROUND

Heart Cakes, Portugal Cakes (page 57) and Queen Cakes (page 61) are all closely related. Like many cakes of the period, Heart Cakes call for brandy to flavour and moisten the batter.

This recipe also uses candied orange and citron peel. Citron is a citrus fruit, similar to a lemon, but larger and with a thick, rough peel. Its flavour is less intense than a lemon's. The peel is the best part of the fruit and is candied to add a mild lemon flavour to baking. The lemon-like citron should not be confused with the citron melon, a variety of watermelon whose rind was also candied and was used as a substitute for citron in recipes.

1½ cups (375 mL) currants

1 cup (250 mL) unsalted butter, softened

1 cup (250 mL) granulated sugar

3 medium eggs, separated

3 medium egg yolks

1¾ cups (435 mL) all-purpose flour

3 Tbsp (45 mL) brandy

2 Tbsp (30 mL) finely chopped candied orange peel

2 Tbsp (30 mL) finely chopped candied citron peel

Grease 12 shallow heart-shaped cake cups and line the bottom of the cups with parchment paper cut to fit.

Soak the currants in hot water for 5 minutes. Drain and spread out to dry on a towel-lined tray, about 15 minutes.

Meanwhile, in a large bowl, beat the butter until fluffy and cream coloured. Beat in the sugar, ⅓ cup (80 mL) at a time, beating until fluffy.

Place the 3 egg whites in a large bowl. Set aside.

In a separate bowl, beat the 6 egg yolks until thick and light coloured. Stir them into the sugar and butter mixture. Stir in the flour in 3 additions, alternating with the brandy in 2 additions. Sprinkle the currants, orange peel and citron peel overtop and gently mix in.

Beat the reserved egg whites to stiff but not dry peaks. Stir about one-third into the batter. Fold in the remainder to make a smooth, even batter. Scrape the batter into the prepared heart-shaped cake cups, smoothing the tops.

Bake in the centre of a 350°F (180°C) oven until the cakes are golden around the edges and firm to the touch, and a toothpick inserted into the centre comes out clean, about 20 minutes. Let cool in the pans for 10 minutes. Loosen the cakes with a blunt knife and turn them onto a rack to cool completely.

(Make-ahead: Layer in an airtight container and store at room temperature for up to a few days, or freeze for up to 2 weeks.)

Makes 12 hearts.

Archeologists found shards of "Blue Italia" Spode china in the vicinity of the officers' kitchens. This china pattern is still in production and was chosen by the Fort curator for the officers' mess dining room.

Portugal Cakes

To a pound of fine flour well dried, add a pound of double refined sugar finely seered; take a pound of new butter, wash it in rose water, and roll it till it is very soft; throw in the sugar and flour by degrees, till half in, working it with your hands; put in the yolks of six eggs, beat the whites with two spoonfuls of sack and work in the other half of the flour; when the oven is hot, put in a pound of currants ready washed and dried; your pan must be ready buttered fill them half full, and scrape some fine sugar over them; the oven must be moderately hot, and set up the stone; you may make them plain.

HISTORIC RECIPE EXCERPTED FROM

The Compleat Confectioner; or The Whole Art of Confectionery Made Plain and Easy

(Hannah Glasse, 1760)

~ PORTUGAL CAKES ~

Flavouring the batter with rosewater replaces the method of washing the butter in rosewater, which was possibly done to freshen the butter and remove some of the salt used to preserve it. Up until the mid-19th century, rosewater and orange flower water were the flavours of choice.

HISTORICAL BACKGROUND

The term "cake" was used to describe small "cup" cakes like these dense, fine-textured Portugal Cakes, as well as larger, rich cakes like A Seed Cake, Very Rich (page 39), which were served in slices, not wedges. The term was also used for what we would now call cookies or biscuits, for example, Shrewsbury Cakes (page 11).

You may wonder why there are three recipes in our collection whose titles include either "Portugal" or "Portuguese." One theory is that Portuguese recipes became popular in British cookbooks due to the Portuguese wife of Charles II, Catherine of Braganza, who grew to favour English fashion but retained a preference for Portuguese food and recipes. Other countries like France, Spain, the Netherlands and Germany also influenced British cooks and their cookbooks. Our inclusion of recipes connected to Portugal reflects how popular they were among cooks at that time.

·⟨⟩——————⟩·

1 cup (250 mL) currants

2 cups (500 mL) all-purpose flour

1 cup (250 mL) granulated sugar

1 cup (250 mL) unsalted butter, cubed and softened

3 medium eggs, separated

1 Tbsp (15 mL) rosewater

1 Tbsp (15 mL) sherry

2 Tbsp (30 mL) superfine granulated sugar

Grease 12 muffin cups and line the bottom of the cups with parchment paper cut to fit.

Soak the currants in hot water for 5 minutes. Drain and spread out to dry on a towel-lined tray, about 15 minutes.

In a large bowl, whisk together the flour and sugar. Sprinkle the butter overtop and work it in with your fingertips or a pastry blender until the mixture is crumbly. Stir in the currants.

In a separate bowl, beat the egg yolks until very thick and light coloured, about 5 minutes.

In another bowl, beat the egg whites with the rosewater and sherry until firm, glossy peaks form.

Stir the beaten yolks into the flour mixture. Spoon about one-third of the egg white mixture over the flour mixture and stir to combine. Fold in the remaining egg white mixture to make a smooth batter. Scrape into the prepared muffin cups, smoothing the tops. Sprinkle the superfine sugar over the batter.

Bake the cakes in the centre of a 350°F (180°C) oven until light golden around the edges and a toothpick inserted into the centre comes out clean, 30 to 40 minutes. Let cool in the pan on a rack for 10 minutes. Loosen the cakes with a blunt knife and turn out, right-side up, onto a rack to cool completely.

(Make-ahead: Layer in an airtight container. Store at room temperature for up to a few days, or freeze for up to 2 weeks.)

Makes 12 small cakes.

Queen Cakes

TAKE a pound of loaf sugar, beat and sift it, a pound of flour well dried, a pound of butter, eight eggs, half a pound of currants washed and picked, grate a nutmeg, the same quantity of mace and cinnamon. Work your butter to a cream, then put in your sugar, beat the whites of your eggs near half an hour, mix them with your sugar and butter. Then beat your yolks near half an hour and put them to your butter, beat them exceedingly well together. Then put in your flour, spices, and the currants. When it is ready for the oven bake them in tins and dust a little sugar over them.

HISTORIC RECIPE EXCERPTED FROM
The Experienced English Housekeeper
(Elizabeth Raffald, 1769)

~ QUEEN CAKES ~

*These cakes were originally baked in fluted tin moulds,
often in fancy shapes such as hearts. Extra ingredients, such as chopped
almonds and grated lemon rind, were sometimes added for variety. When
Fort York hosts citizenship ceremonies for new Canadians, the reception
afterwards often features a selection of small cakes like Queen Cakes,
Portugal Cakes (page 57) and Little Fine Cakes (page 49).*

HISTORICAL BACKGROUND

Recipes for "queen cakes" appear in many 18th- and 19th-century cookery books. "Queen" was a generic term for little cakes (sponge, fruit or pound cakes). They were often dusted with sugar just before going into the oven, or were iced or glazed with a mixture of beaten egg white, sugar and rosewater, applied with a fine feather brush just after they came out of the oven.

· ⊏━━━━━━━━━━ ⊐ ·

1 cup (250 mL) currants

2 cups (500 mL) unsalted butter, softened

2 cups (500 mL) granulated sugar

8 medium eggs, separated

3 cups (750 mL) all-purpose flour

2 tsp (10 mL) ground cinnamon

2 tsp (10 mL) ground mace

2 tsp (10 mL) grated nutmeg

2 Tbsp (30 mL) superfine granulated sugar

Grease 24 muffin cups and line the bottoms of the cups with parchment paper cut to fit.

Soak the currants in hot water for 5 minutes. Drain and spread out to dry on a towel-lined tray, about 15 minutes.

In a large bowl, beat the butter and sugar until very light and fluffy.

In a separate bowl, beat the egg yolks until thick and light coloured, about 5 minutes. Stir into the butter mixture. Set aside the egg whites.

In another bowl, whisk together the flour, cinnamon, mace and nutmeg. Stir into the butter mixture, 1 cup (250 mL) at a time, to make a smooth batter. Sprinkle the currants over the batter.

In a clean bowl, beat the reserved egg whites to stiff, glossy, moist peaks. Stir about one-third of the whites, with the currants, into the batter. Fold in the remaining egg whites. Scrape into the prepared muffin cups, tapping the pan on the work surface to eliminate any air bubbles, and smooth the top. Sprinkle the superfine sugar over the batter.

Bake in the centre of a 350°F (180°C) oven until the cakes come away from the edges of the muffin cups, and a toothpick inserted into the centre comes out clean, about 35 minutes. Let cool in the pans on a rack for 20 minutes. Loosen the edges of the cakes with a blunt knife and turn out onto the rack to cool completely.

(Make-ahead: Layer cakes in an airtight container and store at room temperature for up to a few days. Or freeze for up to 2 weeks.)

Makes 24 small cakes.

Derby or Short Cakes

RUB one pound of butter into two pounds of sifted flour, put one pound of currants, one pound of sugar, mix all together with half a pint of milk, one egg, two teaspoonfuls of pearlash, roll it out thin; cut it in round cakes and bake them.

HISTORIC RECIPE EXCERPTED FROM
The Cook Not Mad; Or, Rational Cookery
(Anonymous, 1831)

~ DERBY OR SHORT CAKES ~

Derby cakes are sheer fun to make with young visitors in
the 1826 kitchen. The staff and volunteer historical cooks invite them to
mix up the dough, roll it out on the big wooden table, cut out the rounds,
and then, depending on their age, help turn the scone-like cakes over
as they bake on the large, oval cast-iron griddle (see photo page 66).
Derby cakes are at their most tempting while still warm.

HISTORICAL BACKGROUND

Derby (pronounced *DAR-bee*) is a small city in the East Midlands, England. Derby cakes (or short cakes) are one of many examples of regional
griddle cakes found throughout the British Isles. Since the Middle Ages,
bakers have used the term "short" to mean a dough with a high ratio
of fat to flour so that the resulting baked cakes are crumbly and tender.
Several 18th- and 19th-century cookbooks include similar recipes for
Derby cakes. In Dr. Kitchener's *The Cook's Oracle,* published in 1830,
the recipe contains no pearlash and he specifies that the cakes are to be
baked in an oven. We prefer the older method of baking them on the
griddle because it makes them more moist and tender.

1 cup (250 mL) currants

3½ cups (875 mL) all-purpose flour

1 tsp (5 mL) baking soda

1 cup (250 mL) unsalted butter, cubed

1 cup (250 mL) granulated sugar

1 medium egg yolk

½ cup (125 mL) whole milk

Soak the currants in hot water for 5 minutes. Drain and spread out to dry on a towel-lined tray, about 15 minutes.

In a large bowl, whisk together the flour and baking soda. Using a pastry blender or your fingertips, work the butter into the dry ingredients until the mixture resembles fresh breadcrumbs. Mix in the sugar and the currants.

Whisk together the egg yolk and milk. Make a well in the centre of the dry ingredients and pour in the milk mixture. With a fork, combine all the ingredients to make a soft, but not sticky, dough. Dust your hands with flour if necessary to handle the dough easily. Divide the dough in half. Place a bowl over one half of the dough while you are working with the other.

On a well-floured work surface, roll out the dough, one half at a time, to a scant ¼-inch (6 mm) thickness. Use a 2½-inch (6 cm) cutter to cut out rounds, dipping the cutter into flour if necessary to prevent sticking. Reroll the scraps to make more rounds.

(Make-ahead: Layer the rounds with waxed or parchment paper in airtight containers and freeze for up to 2 weeks. Thaw before baking.)

Bake on a griddle or cast iron skillet over medium-low to medium heat until golden on the bottom, about 5 minutes. Bake on the second side until golden and the cakes are cooked through, about 4 minutes. Keep the heat moderate or the outside of the Derby Cakes will darken or burn before the insides are cooked.

Makes about 45 cakes.

❀   ❀   ❀   ❀

TIP The recipe above is half the size of the original, which called for 1 egg. For this half-size recipe, you can use the yolk of a medium egg, or beat the whole egg and add half to the dough, saving the rest for another dish.

The 1815 Officers' Brick Barracks and mess establishment. The mess dining room is to the left of the entrance. To the right are the mess sergeant's rooms; behind are the mess kitchen and bake oven (far right).

Chocolate Cream

TAKE a Quart of Cream, a Pint of white Wine, and a little Juice of Lemon; sweeten it very well, lay in a Sprig of Rosemary, grate some Chocolate, and mix all together; stir them over the Fire till it is thick, and pour it into your Cups.

HISTORIC RECIPE EXCERPTED FROM

The Compleat Confectioner; or The Whole Art of Confectionery Made Plain and Easy

(Hannah Glasse, 1760)

~ CHOCOLATE CREAM ~

While very chocolaty, this "cream" is not thick like modern chocolate puddings. It's more like a pouring custard, and is a very elegant dessert to serve in small pot de crème dishes, demi-tasse cups or ramekins.

HISTORICAL BACKGROUND

Chocolate was initially served as a drink, but in the mid-18th century cooks began to include it in desserts. Hannah Glasse was one of the first English cooks to use chocolate in this way. Cream was always the base for "creams" to which various flavourings such as lemon, orange, pistachio, raspberry, strawberry, coffee and, of course, chocolate were added.

We suspect that officers at Fort York might have indulged in chocolate desserts, as Quetton St. George, a merchant in the town of York, in 1803 in the *Upper Canada Gazette,* advertised chocolate "of two qualities" imported from New York.

1 cup (250 mL) fruity white wine, such as Riesling

¼ cup (60 mL) granulated sugar

2 tsp (10 mL) fresh lemon juice

2 cups (500 mL) whipping cream

4 oz (125 g) unsweetened chocolate, finely chopped

One 4-inch (10 cm) sprig fresh rosemary

In a heavy-bottomed saucepan, stir together the wine, sugar and lemon juice until the sugar dissolves. Stir in the whipping cream, chocolate and rosemary.

Cook over medium heat, whisking constantly, until the chocolate melts and the mixture comes to a simmer. Simmer until it coats the back of a metal spoon, about 5 to 10 minutes. Strain through a fine mesh sieve and pour into small pot de crème cups. Let cool, then cover and refrigerate.

(Make-ahead: Refrigerate for up to 2 days.)

Makes 8 small but amazing servings.

~ SOLID SYLLABUBS ~

*Initially a syllabub was a festive drink of wine,
cider or beer mixed with sweetened milk and flavoured with spices such
as cinnamon and nutmeg. Over the years, cream replaced milk, and wine
became the only alcohol in the drink. This was called whipped syllabub.
The next development, the "everlasting" syllabub, reduced
the ratio of alcohol to cream. This almost solid syllabub could stand for a
long time without separating and was a dessert rather than a drink. Our
modern version of a solid syllabub (pictured in the photo on page 8)
is based on a recipe in Hannah Glasse's*
The Art of Cookery Made Plain and Easy.

OUR MODERN EQUIVALENT

4 cups (1 L) cold whipping cream

1 cup (250 mL) granulated sugar

2 cups (500 mL) fruity white wine, such as Riesling

2 lemons, juice of 2, grated rind (zest) of 1

Beat the cream until it forms soft peaks. Gradually add the sugar, then
the wine, lemon juice and lemon rind. Continue beating until the
cream holds peaks. Spoon into small individual wine glasses.

Makes 20 servings. For a more modest number of servings, divide
the ingredients in half.

Burnt Cream

BOIL a pint of cream with a stick of cinnamon, and some lemon peel; take it off the fire, and pour it very slowly into the yelks of four eggs, stirring till half cold, sweeten, and take out the spice, &c; put it into the dish; when cold, strew white pounded sugar over, and brown it with a salamander.

HISTORIC RECIPE EXCERPTED FROM

A New System of Domestic Cookery,
Formed Upon the Principles of Economy

(Maria Eliza Rundell, 1806) ·

~ BURNT CREAM ~

*The staff and volunteer cooks like a culinary challenge, especially
when the Fort opens its doors for events like Best Before 1812, a bicentennial
food symposium showcasing historical foods of the First Nations, British
and Americans. Burnt cream, commonly known by its French name,
crème brûlée, has delighted guests at the Best Before 1812 event, pleased the
dancers at Queen Charlotte's Birthday Ball (a January gala occasion) and
earned requests for seconds at Mad for Marmalade (a popular
Fort event held every February).*

HISTORICAL BACKGROUND

Many believe that this dessert was popularized by Trinity College,
Cambridge, in the late 19th century, but its associations with Britain go
back much further. Burnt cream is the English term for crème brûlée,
which was first introduced to Britain by the French cook Massialot in
1702. The caramelized sugar topping on the custard was described by
British cookbook writer Elizabeth Raffald in *The Experienced Housewife* as looking "like a glass plate put over your cream." A salamander
(see photo page 77) is a round or square piece of iron with an iron-
rod handle, sometimes with feet. In the days before broilers and kitchen
blowtorches, it was heated until red hot over the coals and held over the
sugared custards to caramelize the sugar.

·⊂————※————⊃·

2 cups (500 mL) whipping cream

¼ cup (60 mL) granulated sugar

1 cinnamon stick, broken in half

Finely pared rind from 1 lemon

4 medium egg yolks

1 tsp (5 mL) granulated sugar, for sprinkling

In a heavy-bottomed saucepan, stir together the cream, sugar, cinnamon and lemon rind. Over medium heat, bring to a boil, stirring often. Remove from the heat and let steep until cool, about 40 minutes.

Remove the cinnamon and pour the liquid into a medium-size heatproof bowl. Whisk in the egg yolks. Set the bowl over a saucepan of simmering water, ensuring that the water does not touch the bowl. Cook, stirring often, until the mixture is thick enough to coat the back of a metal spoon, about 15 minutes.

Strain through a fine mesh sieve and pour into 6 to 8 small ramekins or heatproof dessert bowls, each large enough to hold about ⅓ cup (80 mL). Chill until firm.

(Make-ahead: Cover and refrigerate for up to 2 days.)

Place the ramekins on a rimmed baking sheet. Sprinkle the 1 tsp (5 mL) sugar evenly over each custard. With a small blowtorch, heat the sugar topping until melted, bubbling and golden brown, about 30 seconds to 1 minute per ramekin.

(Make-ahead: Refrigerate, uncovered, for up to 2 hours.)

Makes 6 to 8 deliciously creamy, crackling burnt creams.

A red-hot salamander (see the historical background to the recipe) after a lengthy heating in the coals

Rice Pudding with Fruit

SWELL the rice with a very little milk over the fire, then mix fruit of any kind with it (currants; gooseberries scalded; pared and quartered apples; raisins, or black currants;) with one egg into the rice, to bind it; boil it well, and serve with sugar.

HISTORIC RECIPE EXCERPTED FROM

A New System of Domestic Cookery,
Formed Upon the Principles of Economy

(Maria Eliza Rundell, 1806)

～ RICE PUDDING WITH FRUIT ～

*Short-grain rice, preferably an Italian rice such as arborio,
produces a sweet, velvety rice pudding studded with raisins, currants and
chunks of apple. Adding the milk in stages, like the technique for risotto,
results in a remarkably creamy dessert.*

HISTORICAL BACKGROUND

This recipe is descended from medieval rice pottage, a thick mixture of
boiled rice mixed with milk. In the early 19th century, rice puddings
continued to be baked in an oven or boiled like this recipe, over a fire.
The rice could be whole or ground, and the puddings could be sweetened with sugar enriched with eggs, especially yolks, and flavoured with
spices like nutmeg and cinnamon, currants, lemon or flower waters.

Rice was an important component of military rations in Upper
Canada. Soldiers received 1¹⁄₇ ounces (about 32 g) daily while in gar-
rison and would never have made a pudding with this ration, instead
using it to thicken and enrich their stews. In the officers' mess, however,
a sweet rice pudding would have been enjoyed at dinner.

OUR MODERN EQUIVALENT

⅓ cup (80 mL) arborio or other short-grain rice

4 cups (1 L) whole milk (approximate)

¼ cup (60 mL) currants

¼ cup (60 mL) raisins

1 apple, peeled, cored and diced (any type of apple works well)

1 medium egg

Granulated sugar, for sprinkling

In a heavy-bottomed medium saucepan, combine the rice with 2 cups (500 mL) of the milk. Bring to a simmer, stirring, over medium heat. Reduce the heat to low and cook at a very gentle simmer, stirring regularly, until the rice expands, about 15 minutes. Stir in 1 cup (250 mL) of the remaining milk. Cook, stirring, and, after about 15 minutes, as the pudding thickens, stir in the remaining 1 cup (250 mL) of milk. Cook, stirring regularly, until the rice is tender and the pudding thickened, about 10 minutes.

Meanwhile, rinse the currants and raisins and stir them into the rice mixture. Cook, stirring a few times, for 5 minutes. Add the apple and cook until it is tender, about 5 minutes.

In a bowl, whisk the egg, then mix in about ½ cup (125 mL) of the pudding. Whisk this back into the saucepan and cook, stirring, for 2 minutes, adding a little more milk if needed to thin the pudding. Remove from the heat.

(Make-ahead: Let cool. Transfer to an airtight container. Cover the surface directly with plastic wrap and refrigerate for up to 2 days. When reheating, add a bit of milk to loosen the rice.)

Scoop into individual bowls and serve with sugar sprinkled overtop. You may find that the fruit sweetens the pudding enough that sugar is not needed.

Makes about 6 servings.

❀   ❀   ❀   ❀

TIP The only raisins available in the Georgian era came from dried grapes with seeds. Before mixing up any batter, cooks had to remove the seeds from each raisin—a laborious task. No wonder currants, dried small black raisins with seeds so small they didn't need to be removed, were the dried fruit of choice. You can still find these old-fashioned raisins—Lexia or Muscat, for example—although it might require some effort. They are a blessing for bakers, as they have been mechanically seeded. Nowadays, almost all the raisins in the supermarket are sultanas, dried seedless grapes, from varieties developed later in the 19th century.

Bread and Butter Pudding

TAKE a Penny-loaf and cut it into thin Slices of Bread and Butter as you do for Tea. Butter your Dish as you cut them, lay Slices all over the Dish, then strew a few Currans clean washed and picked, then a row of bread and butter, then a few currans clean washed and picked, then a Row of Bread and butter, then a few currans, and so on till all your Bread and Butter is in; then take a Pint of Milk, beat up four Eggs, a little Salt, half a Nutmeg grated, mix all together with Sugar to your Taste; Pour this over the Bread, and bake it half an Hour. A puff paste under does best. You may put in two Spoonfuls of Rose-water.

HISTORIC RECIPE EXCERPTED FROM
The Art of Cookery Made Plain and Easy
(Hannah Glasse, 1747)

~ BREAD AND BUTTER PUDDING ~

On special occasion days like Battle of York Day (April 27) and Simcoe Day (the first Monday in August), volunteer historical cooks invite visitors to sample some of the authentic dishes of the period of the Fort. This is one of the recipes that always appeals not only to the adults but also to the children, who often get to help butter the bread and layer it with the currants and custard in the baking dish. Helpers are always first to sample this simple but delicious pudding. Bread and Butter Pudding takes on a special occasion aura when prepared for the Friends of Fort York annual Directors' Dinner.

HISTORICAL BACKGROUND

"Ah, what an excellent thing is an English Pudding! To come in pudding-time, is as much as to say, to come in the most lucky moment in the world. Give an Englishman a pudding, and he shall think it a noble treat in any part of the world," declared French visitor Monsieur Maximilien Misson in 1691.

Among the numerous puddings, those including bread were very popular. Bread and butter pudding was not as common as plain bread pudding. The latter was made with breadcrumbs or grated bread with milk or cream, eggs, sugar and sometimes currants or raisins—no butter. Some culinary historians speculate that bread and butter puddings are related to whitepots/whitpots, which are puddings containing slices of bread with milk or cream, eggs, sugar, spices and dried fruit, with a little butter added. It was a simple step from adding butter to buttering the bread.

In this recipe Hannah Glasse tells us that the bread should be sliced "as you do for tea." Thinly sliced buttered bread was often served with tea.

OUR MODERN EQUIVALENT

2 Tbsp (30 mL) butter, softened (approximate)

½ cup (125 mL) currants

12 thin slices good quality dense white bread

4 medium eggs

2 cups (500 mL) whole milk

¼ cup (60 mL) granulated sugar

2 Tbsp (30 mL) rosewater

¼ tsp (1 mL) grated nutmeg

Pinch salt

Lightly grease the bottom and sides of an 8-inch (2 L) square baking dish with some of the butter.

Rinse the currants in warm water. Drain and set aside.

Trim off the bread crusts and use the rest of the butter to butter the bread on one side. Arrange 4 slices of the bread, buttered-side up, over the bottom of the prepared baking dish. Sprinkle half of the currants over the bread. Repeat with another layer of bread and currants, then a final layer of bread.

In a large bowl, whisk the eggs. Whisk in the milk, sugar, rosewater, nutmeg and salt. Pour over the layered bread and let stand for 30 minutes.

(Make-ahead: Cover and refrigerate for up to 8 hours.)

Press the top of the pudding lightly to make sure the top layer of bread is moist.

Bake in the centre of a 350°F (180°C) oven until puffed and golden, and a thin knife inserted into the centre comes out clean, about 45 minutes.

Makes 6 to 8 servings.

❀　❀　❀　❀

TIP For best results, buy an uncut loaf of dense white bread and cut thinly into slices about ¼ inch (6 mm) thick. Slightly stale bread is fine, in fact, better.

Ginger Ice Cream

TAKE four ounces of ginger preserved, pound it and put it in a bason, with 2 gills of syrup, a lemon squeezed, and one pint of cream; then freeze it.

HISTORIC RECIPE EXCERPTED FROM

*The Complete Confectioner;
or The Whole Art of Confectionery*

(Frederick Nutt, 1789)

~ GINGER ICE CREAM ~

Two of the foods in the historical kitchen that elicit the greatest surprise—
and wows—are chocolate (see the Chocolate Cream on page 71) and ice
cream. A combination of ice and salt was used to freeze custards and
fruit mixtures into ice cream and sorbets, decades before the advent of
electric freezers. Two "gills" of syrup are 1 cup (250 mL).

HISTORICAL BACKGROUND

The first English recipe for ice cream is found in *Mrs. Mary Eales's Receipts,* from 1718. Elizabeth Raffald has a recipe in her 1769 edition of *The Experienced English Housekeeper* for an "ice cream made with 12 ripe apricots," and gives the option to use "any sort of fruit if you have not apricots." Ice cream was well known in Italy and France at that time, but did not become popular until later in the century in England. The author of this recipe, Frederick Nutt, was an apprentice of an Italian confectioner named Domenico Negri, who had a shop in Berkeley Square, London, in the 1760s called The Pot and Pineapple. (In the Georgian era, the pineapple was a symbol used for confectioners' shops.) Nutt includes 32 ice creams and 24 ice recipes in his confectionery book.

In the late 18th century, ice cream was made by filling a wooden pail or pewter pan with ice and salt. The ice cream was put into a sarbotiere (a cylindrical pot with a lid) and plunged into the salt/ice mixture. The sarbotiere was then turned and agitated in the ice. The lid was periodically removed and the ice cream stirred to prevent large ice crystals from forming. The sarbotiere remained in the ice until the ice cream became firm. The ice cream was then removed from the sarbotiere and sometimes put into pewter moulds and frozen again in ice and salt. It was served in a porcelain or ceramic ice pail or in glasses.

OUR MODERN EQUIVALENT

¾ cup (185 mL) water

¾ cup (185 mL) granulated sugar

½ cup (125 mL) mashed or very finely minced preserved ginger, lightly packed (4 oz/125 g)

Juice of 1 lemon

2 cups (500 mL) whipping cream

In a saucepan, bring the water and sugar to a boil, stirring to dissolve the sugar. Boil for 4 minutes, then pour the syrup into a large heatproof bowl to cool to room temperature.

Whisk in the ginger and lemon juice. Add the cream, stirring just until blended. Refrigerate, uncovered, until cold.

Freeze in an ice cream machine according to the manufacturer's instructions. Alternatively, scrape the ginger mixture into a shallow metal cake pan and freeze, uncovered, until almost all frozen. Break it into chunks and, working with half of the chunks at a time, whirl in a food processor until smooth. Scrape into an airtight container and

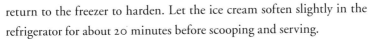

return to the freezer to harden. Let the ice cream soften slightly in the refrigerator for about 20 minutes before scooping and serving.

(Make-ahead: Cover surface directly with plastic wrap. Store in the freezer for up to 4 days. If ice crystals develop in the ice cream, rewhirl in the food processor and refreeze.)

Makes 4 cups (1 L) ice cream, enough for 8 servings.

❀ ❀ ❀ ❀

TIP Look for ginger preserved in syrup for this ice cream. It is often labelled "stem ginger," with "stem" signifying that the ginger is young and tender. If all you can find is crystallized ginger, choose pliant thick slices of ginger and rinse off the sugar before mashing.

A woodcut of a sarbotiere. This image is from culinary historian
Ivan Day's *Ice Cream*; it originally appeared in M. Emy's
L'Art de bien faire les glaces d'office (1768).

Negus Ice

A BOTTLE of port wine, half a nutmeg grated, the zest of a lemon rubbed off on sugar, a pint of syrup or more to taste: freeze this.

HISTORIC RECIPE EXCERPTED FROM
The Cook and Housewife's Manual
(Margaret Dods, 1833)

~ NEGUS ICE ~

A very sophisticated moulded ice, Negus Ice has proved to be a winner at the Fort's Queen Charlotte Ball when it is served to the dancers taking a break from the reels and cotillions. Negus Ice, nicknamed "port-sicles" at the Fort, is delicious as a dessert, a palate cleanser or a simple refreshment on a hot day.

HISTORICAL BACKGROUND

In the 18th and early 19th centuries, it became fashionable in England to flavour ices with liqueurs.

This port-based ice recipe derives its name from a drink, Negus, which was created by an English colonel named Francis Negus. He was the Commissioner for Executing the Office of Master of the Horse from 1717 until 1727, and then Master of the Buckhounds. The drink, which was served warm, includes the same ingredients as the ice, but with the addition of burgundy wine and brandy.

In the late 18th and early 19th centuries ice was available in York. It was harvested from Lake Ontario and other small lakes and ponds and stored in ice houses. Elizabeth Simcoe, wife of Lieutenant Governor John Graves Simcoe, remarked while in Montreal in 1792 that "Ice houses are very general here but seldom for the purpose of furnishing Ice for a dessert. They use the Ice to cool Liquors & butter & the ice houses are used for Larders to keep meat." The officers at Fort York likely used the ice available in a similar manner. In the 1820s the officers requested their own ice house, to be built with government funds, but their request was denied.

OUR MODERN EQUIVALENT

2 cups (500 mL) water

1 cup (250 mL) granulated sugar

4 cups (1 L) ruby port

1 Tbsp (15 mL) grated lemon rind (zest)

½ tsp (2 mL) grated nutmeg

In a saucepan, bring the water and sugar to a boil, stirring to dissolve the sugar. When the syrup clears, pour it into a large heatproof bowl and let cool to room temperature.

Mix in the port, lemon rind and nutmeg.

Pour the liquid into small moulds or cups that hold about ¼ cup (60 mL) each, or larger if desired. Arrange on a tray, cover and freeze until firm, about 4 hours.

(Make-ahead: Freeze for up to 3 days.)

Makes 24 mini port-sicles.

Pears Portuguese Fashion with Currants

TAKE three or four boncretiens, or other good winter pears, pare them, cut them in two, and take out the choke, boil them in water only half an hour, put them into a stewpan, pour in a pint of port wine, with a lump of fine sugar, a stick of cinnamon, a bit of lemon peel, a spoonful or two of water, and about five or six ounces of the best dry currants; let all stew together till your pears are very tender; dish them up, and pour your currants over, but take out the cinnamon and peel.

HISTORIC RECIPE EXCERPTED FROM

A Complete System of Cookery

(William Verral, 1759)

PEARS PORTUGUESE FASHION WITH CURRANTS

A timeless fruit dessert that's as handsome and stylish on the table today as it was in 1759. In today's kitchen, look for Bartlett, Bosc or Anjou pears.

HISTORICAL BACKGROUND

A "boncretien" is an 18th-century English pear variety that is said to be "preferable to all other pears to be stew'd or baked," according to the *Dictionaire Oeconomique,* 1725. They were a winter variety that stored well; the modern version of this variety is the Bartlett.

Port was subject to lower tariffs and so it became the cheapest foreign wine. French wines had previously been popular (in Britain and its then colony Canada) but with worsening relations with France, port wine (Portuguese red wine fortified with brandy) became a patriotic drink and was used in many recipes. A hero of the War of 1812, General Issac Brock had a barrel of port wine listed among his possessions after his death at the Battle of Queenston Heights in 1813.

6 pears, about 3 lb (1.5 kg)

4 cups (1 L) water

2 cups (500 mL) ruby port

¾ cup (185 mL) currants, rinsed

½ cup (125 mL) granulated sugar

1 cinnamon stick, broken in half

Thinly pared rind of 1 lemon

Peel, halve and core the pears. In a large, wide saucepan, bring the water to a boil, then add the pears. Cover and simmer until very slightly softened, about 10 minutes. Reserving 1 cup (250 mL) of the poaching liquid, drain the pears.

In the same saucepan, bring the reserved poaching liquid, port, currants, sugar, cinnamon and lemon peel to a boil over medium-high heat. Add the partially poached pears. Cover the pears with a round of parchment paper cut to fit overtop. Put the lid on the saucepan. Bring to a boil, then reduce the heat and simmer gently, turning the pears halfway through cooking, until tender but not mushy, 12 to 15 minutes. Let cool in the cooking liquid. Remove the cinnamon.

(Make-ahead: Transfer to an airtight container and refrigerate for up to 2 days.)

Remove the lemon rind. Serve the pears in stemmed glasses or bowls, with a generous amount of the syrup and currants.

Makes 6 generous servings.

Stewed Apples, the Portuguese Way

Take out the Cores, and prick the Skin with the Point of a Knife, and put them in a Dish, or Patty-pan, put some Sugar in the Hollow of your Apples, and a little Water at the Bottom of your Dish, or Patty pan, put them in an Oven, and when they have taken Colour, serve them up hot.

You may put in some Apricot Marmalade. They must also be cut in Halves, and put in a Patty pan, with Half a Pint of Wine and some Sugar, and a little Lemon-peel.

HISTORIC RECIPE EXCERPTED FROM
The Lady's Companion
(Anonymous, 1753)

STEWED APPLES, THE PORTUGUESE WAY

While the recipe title clearly says "stewed," these apples are actually baked in a rather luxurious way with apricot jam and white wine. Almost any apple will work. Empire, Cortland, Spartan and McIntosh are good examples, as is Northern Spy, a premium baking apple discovered in New York State in the early 19th century.

HISTORICAL BACKGROUND

There are many examples of baked or stewed apple recipes in the cookbooks of our time period. In *The Experienced Housekeeper*, 1769, Elizabeth Raffald includes a recipe called To Make Black Caps. In it she brushes the apples with rosewater, grates a little sugar over them and bakes them "till they look bright and very black." She serves them in a dish with either thick cream custard or white wine and sugar. She also has a recipe for Green Caps in which she finishes the apples with the following instruction: "Stick single flowers in every apple and serve them up."

·⊂━━━━━✕✕━━━━━⊃·

6 apples, about 2½ lb (1.25 kg) (any type of apple is fine)
½ cup (125 mL) apricot jam (Marmalade of Apricots, page 115)
1 cup (250 mL) white wine

Cut the apples in half crosswise and cut out the cores. Prick the skins twice with a fork. Arrange, cut-side down, in a shallow baking dish large enough to hold them in one layer.

Spoon jam into the hollows of the apples, then drizzle the wine evenly overtop. Bake, uncovered, in the centre of a 375°F (190°C) oven, basting the apples a few times, until the skins are burnished, the apples are tender and the wine has formed a syrup, about 1½ hours.

Makes 6 servings.

❀　❀　❀　❀

TIP Add a little water, up to ½ cup (125 mL), if the wine evaporates before the apples are tender.

A table set for a Georgian-era dessert course in the officers' mess dining room

Short Paste for Tarts

TAKE a pound of wheat flour, and rub it very small, three quarters of a pound of butter, rub it as small as the flour, put to it three spoonfuls of loaf sugar beat and sifted, take the yolks of four eggs, and beat them very well; put to them a spoonful or two of rosewater, work them to a paste, then roll them thin, and ice them over as you did the other if you please, and bake 'em in a slow oven.

HISTORIC RECIPE EXCERPTED FROM

English Housewifry. Exemplified In above Four Hundred and Fifty Receipts, Giving Directions in most Parts of Cookery

(Elizabeth Moxon, 1764)

~ SHORT PASTE FOR TARTS ~

*This outstanding pastry, one of the Fort's most requested recipes,
is easy to put together, a dream to roll out and so tender. It is the pastry
of choice for rhubarb, strawberry, apple and apricot tarts served at Fort
occasions. However, where this pastry stars is in small tart shells, made in
the hundreds for public events and filled with Red Strawberry Jam
(page III), Marmalade of Apricots (page 115), Marmalade of Peaches
(page 119) or any of the other historical jams, like damson plum, pear and
quince, all made in the Fort's kitchen.*

HISTORICAL BACKGROUND

The egg yolks and butter make this a very rich shortcrust pastry that
would have been used for making tarts. Tarts in the 18th century were
not the small individual tarts we know now in North America. They
were large, uncovered and typically filled with fruit or custard. In this
period small tarts were filled with jam, like the Fort York Jam Tarts
(page 105).

·⟨⟩·

3½ cups (875 mL) all-purpose flour

¼ cup (60 mL) granulated sugar

1½ cups (375 mL) cold butter, cubed

4 medium egg yolks

3 Tbsp (45 mL) rosewater

In a large bowl, whisk together the flour and sugar. Add the butter and, with a pastry cutter or your fingertips, work in the butter until the mixture is crumbly.

In a small bowl, whisk together the egg yolks and rosewater. Drizzle over the crumbs, tossing with a fork until a ragged dough forms. Press together until smooth and shape into 3 discs.

(Make-ahead: Wrap and chill until firm, about 30 minutes or up to 1 day. You can also freeze the dough until needed. Thaw in the refrigerator and let soften slightly before rolling.)

Makes enough pastry for three 9-inch (23 cm) pie shells, or for 6 to 7 dozen small tart shells (depending on the size of tart pan used).

∾ FORT YORK JAM TARTS ∾

*This is not a historical recipe, but we couldn't resist
including it as an example of how to use the pastry. The tarts made
at Fort York are small and shallow, about 2 inches (5 cm) across, not quite
miniature, but no more than two bites. They are made in tart pans, which
have shallower and more rounded sides than muffin pans.*

1 batch Short Paste for Tarts (see page 103)
Jam or marmalade for filling (see recipes pages 111–121)

Roll out the pastry, one disc at a time, on a floured work surface to a
scant ¼-inch (6 mm) thickness. With a 2½-inch (6 cm) fluted cutter,
cut out rounds of pastry. Prick 3 times with a fork and fit into small,
shallow tart pans. Reroll the scraps and cut out more rounds.

Bake in the lower third of a 350°F (180°C) oven until pale gold on
the bottom, about 10 minutes. Transfer the pans to racks to let the pastry shells firm up, about 5 minutes. Remove the shells from the pans
and let cool.

(Make-ahead: Layer in airtight containers. Store at room temperature for a few days or freeze for up to 2 weeks.)

To serve, fill the shells with a rounded teaspoon (6 mL) of jam.

Pippin Tart

PARE thin two Seville or China oranges, boil the peel tender, and shred it fine—pare and core twenty apples, put them in a stew pan, and as little water as possible; when half done, add half a pound of sugar, the orange peel and juice; boil till pretty thick. When cold, put it in a shallow dish, or patty pans lined with paste, to turn out, and be eaten cold.

HISTORIC RECIPE EXCERPTED FROM

A New System of Domestic Cookery,
Formed Upon the Principles of Economy

(Maria Eliza Rundell, 1806)

~ PIPPIN TART ~

*Staff and volunteer historical cooks first made this fancy
apple pie for the Georgian Mess Dinner, held every year as a fundraiser for
the Friends of Fort York. Proceeds from the dinner help to
support the Fort's programs, including the Summer Guard, the youthful
corps of costumed soldiers who animate the Fort with fife and drum playing,
precision marching and, the highlight of each day, firing the cannon.*

HISTORICAL BACKGROUND

Pippin apples came from France and were introduced into England
in the 16th century. The term "pippin" came to be used interchange-
ably with "apple." By 1810, in settled southern areas of Upper Canada,
there were orchards bearing an abundance of plums, pears, peaches and
apples.

An early recipe for Pippin Tart appears in *The Family Dictionary*
by William Salmon, 1710. It calls for 2 oranges (but does not specify
Seville or China) pared and boiled, and 20 apples, all cooked in the
same way as in Maria Rundell's later recipe. Throughout the 18th century many more Pippin Tart recipes were published, and it's interesting
to note that they were all copied almost word for word from William
Salmon's. Even *The Cook Not Mad* in 1831 included a similar recipe, but
called it an apple tart. The original recipe has the option of making
one large tart (pie) or smaller individual tarts (tartlets). At the Fort, the
larger tart suits our special occasions.

·⟨⟩·

1 small orange

6 apples, about 2 lb (1 kg) (any type of apple is fine)

⅓ cup (80 mL) water

⅓ cup (80 mL) granulated sugar

⅓ batch Short Paste for Tarts (page 103)

Pare the outer orange rind from the orange. Squeeze out the juice, discarding any seeds, and set the juice aside. Place the rind in a small saucepan and cover generously with water. Cover and bring to a boil, then reduce the heat and simmer gently until very tender, about 1 hour. Drain and shred finely. Set aside.

Meanwhile, peel, core and thinly slice the apples. Place them in a heavy-bottomed saucepan with the ⅓ cup (80 mL) water and bring to a boil. Simmer, covered, over medium-low heat, stirring often, until translucent and very tender, 20 to 30 minutes depending on the variety and freshness of the apples.

Mash the apples, leaving them with some texture. Stir in the sugar, reserved orange juice and shredded peel. Cook, uncovered, over medium heat, stirring almost constantly until golden and very thick. When you draw a spoon over the bottom of the pan, the resulting channel should fill in slowly.

(Make-ahead: Let cool, then refrigerate in an airtight container for up to 3 days.)

On a well-floured work surface, roll out the pastry to a round about

10 inches (25 cm) in diameter. Fit it into a 9-inch (23 cm) tart pan with a removable bottom, easing and pressing the pastry over the bottom and up the side of the pan without stretching it. Trim off the pastry at the rim.

Line the pastry with foil and fill with dried beans, rice or pastry weights. Bake in the bottom third of a 375°F (190°C) oven for 15 minutes. Remove the beans and foil. Prick the pastry a few times over the bottom, then wrap strips of foil over the pastry along the side and along the rim. Bake until the bottom of the crust is set, has lost its sheen and is no longer translucent, about 15 minutes.

Fill the pastry with the apple mixture, and bake until a glossy film forms and the pastry is golden, 25 to 30 minutes. Let cool on a rack. Serve at room temperature.

(Make ahead: Store lightly covered at room temperature for up to 8 hours.)

Makes 6 to 8 servings.

❀ ❀ ❀ ❀

TIP You can bake a Pippin Tart in a regular 9-inch (23 cm) pie plate following the baking instructions above.

Red Strawberry Jam

GATHER the scarlet berries very ripe, bruise them very fine and put them a little juice of strawberries. Beat and sift their weight in sugar, strew it among them and put them in the preserving pan. Set them over a clear slow fire, skim them and boil them twenty minutes. Then put them in pots or glasses for use.

HISTORIC RECIPE EXCERPTED FROM
The Experienced English Housekeeper
(Elizabeth Raffald, 1769)

~ RED STRAWBERRY JAM ~

Fort York's Canteen Museum Store usually has a selection of
Fort-made jams, and this one, as scarlet as Elizabeth Raffald's berries,
is a bestseller. With Canadian-grown day-neutral strawberries, you can
make strawberry jam all summer long with local berries, avoiding the
berry rush of June and early July.

HISTORICAL BACKGROUND

Strawberries are native to Canada. The French explorer Cartier is
thought to have brought strawberry plants from Quebec to France in
1534. It is generally believed that in the mid-18th century the French
cross-bred the Virginia, a North American variety of wild strawberry,
with a Chilean strawberry to create the bigger, more flavourful berry we
know today.

On June 15, 1793, Elizabeth Simcoe mentioned local wild strawberries in her diary: "The Indians brought us strawberries not quite ripe.
Jone's Sister put them in a saucepan with water & sugar & boiled them
& I thought them good with my tea." This would be Upper Canada's
first recorded strawberry jam.

OUR MODERN EQUIVALENT

8 cups (2 L) strawberries (2½ lb/1.25 kg)

6½ cups (1.625 L) granulated sugar

Rinse and hull the berries. In 2 batches, crush the berries with a large fork or potato masher.

In a Dutch oven or large, shallow, heavy-bottomed saucepan, thoroughly stir the strawberries with the sugar. Bring to a boil over high heat, stirring constantly. Boil, skimming off any obvious foam along the side of the pan, until thickened and a small blob of jam wrinkles when placed on a cold plate, about 10 minutes. Repeat boiling and testing if needed. Remove from the heat and skim off any foam.

Fill hot, clean preserving jars to within ¼ inch (6 mm) of the rim. Seal with warmed new discs and clean rings. Arrange on the rack of a boiling water canner and lower the rack into hot water. Ensure that the water sits 1 inch (2.5 cm) above the top of the jars. Cover and bring the water to a boil. Boil for 10 minutes. Turn off the heat, uncover the canner and let the boiling subside for 5 minutes. Remove the jars and let cool for 24 hours on a rack.

Check that the lids have snapped down, refrigerating any jars whose lids have not. The refrigerated jars of jam must be eaten within 3 weeks. Store in a cool, dark, dry spot for up to 1 year.

Makes about 6 (1 cup/250 mL) jars.

Marmalade of Apricots

TAKE the Apricots when of a pale yellow, pare them, and to a Pound of Apricots put three Quarters of a Pound of fine sugar; but you must cut your Apricots in halves. Take out the Stones, slice them thin, beat your Sugar, and put it into your Preserving-Pan with your slic'd Apricots, and four spoonful of Water; boil and scum them, and when they are tender, put them in Glasses.

HISTORIC RECIPE EXCERPTED FROM

Adam's Luxury, and Eve's Cookery; Or, The The Kitchen-Garden Display'd . . . To Which is Added the Physical Virtues of Every Herb and Root

(Anonymous, 1744)

~ MARMALADE OF APRICOTS ~

*Until well into the 19th century, thick spreads were generally
called marmalade, regardless of the kind of fruit they were made of. Hence,
Marmalade of Apricots (page 115) and Marmalade of Peaches (page 119).
The word "jam," sometimes written "giam," came to apply to preserves
made with soft fruit and berries, leaving citrus fruits exclusive rights to the
title "marmalade." This is the marmalade we use at Fort York to sweeten
and flavour Stewed Apples, the Portuguese Way (page 99) and to fill
Fort York Jam Tarts (page 105).*

HISTORICAL BACKGROUND

Cooking apricots with liberal amounts of sugar to make marmalade
was just one of the ways in which cooks preserved fruit for the winter months. Preserves required fine white sugar traditionally sold in
cone-shaped loaves that were nipped or chipped into small chunks
and pounded with a mortar and pestle until smooth. It's interesting to
note that at the beginning of the 18th century, sugar consumption was
approximately 4 lb (1.8 kg) per person per year; this figure had risen
to 13 lb (almost 6 kg) by the end of the century. Sugar became less of a
luxury and a more affordable ingredient in the kitchen.

A wide range of methods was used in preserving. For example, the
anonymous author of *Adam's Luxury, and Eve's Cookery* offers the Marmalade of Apricots recipe plus four other ways of preserving apricots,
including a recipe to preserve green apricots that instructs the cook to

"get your Apricots before the Stones are hard." The recipe for preserving green apricots is one that has been lost. Later in the century another author, Charlotte Mason, in *The Lady's Assistant,* 1787, described 12 ways to preserve apricots, including in brandy; in a codlin (apple) jelly; cooked, puréed and dried in cakes; cut into slices or chips and dried; preserved whole in a syrupy compote; cut in half and candied; and made into a jam. Mrs. Mason's recipes are so clearly written that modern cooks can follow them successfully.

OUR MODERN EQUIVALENT

12 cups (3 L) sliced, pitted fresh apricots (4¾ lb/2.15 kg)
6½ cups (1.625 L) granulated sugar
½ cup (125 mL) water

In a Dutch oven or large, shallow, heavy-bottomed saucepan, thoroughly stir the apricots with the sugar and water. Bring to a boil over high heat, stirring constantly. Boil hard, stirring constantly, until thick, bubbles break noisily on the surface and the apricot mixture has cleared, about 17 minutes. Remove from the heat and test for the setting point. To do this, drop a small blob of marmalade on a cold plate and wait for 1 minute. If the surface wrinkles when nudged by a spoon, the preserve is ready to jar. Skim off any foam. Repeat boiling and testing if needed.

Fill hot, clean preserving jars to within ¼ inch (6 mm) of the rim. Seal with warmed new discs and clean rings. Arrange on the rack of a boiling water canner and lower the rack into hot water. Ensure that the water sits 1 inch (2.5 cm) above the top of the jars. Cover and bring the water to a boil. Boil for 10 minutes. Turn off the heat, uncover the canner and let the boiling subside for 5 minutes. Remove the jars and let cool for 24 hours on a rack.

Check that the lids have snapped down, refrigerating any jars whose lids have not. The refrigerated jars of marmalade must be eaten within 3 weeks. Store the sealed jars in a cool, dark, dry spot for up to 1 year.

Makes about 8 (1 cup/250 mL) jars.

Marmalade of Peaches

PARE ripe Peaches, take out the Stones, put them in a Stewpan with a little Water, and three Quarters of their Weight of fine sugar. Stew them till they are tender, and then mash them (keeping them boiling) till the whole is thick like Paste. Then take it off, put it out in a glazed Plate, and when cold put it in Glasses, and cover them with white Paper.

HISTORIC RECIPE EXCERPTED FROM

Adam's Luxury, and Eve's Cookery; Or, The The Kitchen-Garden Display'd . . . To Which is Added the Physical Virtues of Every Herb and Root

(Anonymous, 1744)

~ MARMALADE OF PEACHES ~

Mid-season free-stone peaches are fragrant, full of flavour and ideal for making preserves. When using preserves to fill tarts, it's always more appealing to have at least two colours, such as red strawberry and golden peach or apricot.

HISTORICAL BACKGROUND

In the 1790s peaches were grown and harvested at the mouth of the Niagara River and were also available in nearby Grimsby. With fresh peaches so close by, the officers at Fort York must have occasionally enjoyed them. Cooks may have preserved them as well.

In that era, the method of sealing jars was different from today's method. This recipe puts the marmalade "in Glasses, and cover[s] them with white Paper." The paper was an 18th-century way of sealing or covering jars for storage. The technique was to first brush a disc of white paper with brandy and place it directly on the surface of the preserve. The next step was to press a larger circle of paper over the top of the glass and a little down the sides. Finally, the cook tied a string tightly around the top of the glass, thus sealing the preserve. Another method was to cover the surface of the preserve with a layer of mutton fat or oil to exclude the air. Another method, more unusual to us, was a stretched pig's bladder tied tightly over the glass. As the pig's bladder dried it contracted and created a tight seal.

OUR MODERN EQUIVALENT

4 lb (1.8 kg) ripe peaches (8 medium peaches)

½ cup (125 mL) water

5⅓ cups (1.3 L) granulated sugar

To peel the peaches, place them in a large heatproof bowl. Cover them with boiling water and let stand for 30 seconds. Drain and immediately chill in very cold water. Drain, peel, slice thickly and remove the stones.

In a Dutch oven or large, shallow, heavy-bottomed saucepan, thoroughly stir the peaches with the water and sugar. Bring to a boil over high heat, stirring constantly. Boil until the peaches are tender and translucent, about 10 minutes.

Remove from the heat and mash the peaches thoroughly with a potato masher. Bring them back to a boil, stirring constantly. Boil until the preserve thickens and a small blob wrinkles on a cold plate, about 10 minutes. Repeat boiling and testing if needed. Skim off any foam.

Fill hot, clean preserving jars to within ¼ inch (6 mm) of the rim. Seal with warmed new discs and clean rings. Arrange on the rack of a boiling water canner and lower the rack into hot water. Ensure that the water sits 1 inch (2.5 cm) above the top of the jars. Cover and bring the water to a boil. Boil for 10 minutes. Turn off the heat, uncover the canner and let the boiling subside for 5 minutes. Remove the jars and let cool for 24 hours on a rack.

Check that the lids have snapped down, refrigerating any jars whose lids have not. The refrigerated jars of marmalade must be eaten within 3 weeks. Store in a cool, dark, dry spot for up to 1 year.

Makes about 6 (1 cup/250 mL) jars.

ADAM's LUXURY,

AND

EVE's COOKERY;

OR, THE

Kitchen-Garden diſplay'd.

In Two Parts.

I. Shewing the beſt and moſt approved Methods of raiſing and bringing to the greateſt Perfection, all the Products of the Kitchen-Garden ; with a Kalendar ſhewing the different Products of each Month, and the Buſineſs proper to be done in it.

II. Containing a large Collection of RECEIPTS for dreſſing all Sorts of Kitchen Stuff, ſo as to afford a great Variety of cheap, healthful, and palatable Diſhes.

To which is Added,

The Phyſical Virtues of every Herb and Root.

Deſigned for the Uſe of all who would live Cheap, and preſerve their Health to old Age ; particularly for Farmers and Tradeſmen in the Country, who have but ſmall Pieces of Garden Ground, and are willing to make the moſt of it.

LONDON:

Printed for R. DODSLEY, in *Pall-Mall* ; and Sold by M. COOPER, at the *Globe* in *Pater-noſter Row.*

MDCCXLIV.

Frontispiece from *Adam's Luxury and Eve's Cookery* (1744), a favourite cookbook for fruit and vegetable recipes

Another Excellent Lemonade

TAKE one gallon of water, put it to the juice of ten good lemons, and the zest of six of them likewise, then add to this one pound of sugar, and mix it well together, strain it through a fine strainer, and put it in ice to cool; this will be a most delicious and fine lemonade.

HISTORIC RECIPE EXCERPTED FROM
The House Servant's Directory
(Robert Roberts, 1827)

~ ANOTHER EXCELLENT LEMONADE ~

*Lemonade has never lost its appeal, especially in the summer.
When groups of visitors finish their tour of the Fort in the historical kitchen,
they often have the chance to sample this excellent lemonade. One of the
common questions asked is whether the officers' kitchen would have
had lemons. Many recipes of the period featured lemons, and we know for
certain that lemon juice was available in York in 1803.*

*The full name of the original recipe is "Another Excellent
Lemonade, by R.R., the Author of This Book." We've only included one
lemonade recipe in* Setting a Fine Table, *but the source book,* The House
Servant's Directory, *contains no fewer than four lemonade recipes.*

HISTORICAL BACKGROUND

Lemonade was a popular non-alcoholic beverage in the 19th century.
Early lemonades were made with real lemon peel or zest, juice, sugar
and water. The ingredients were allowed to steep to concentrate the flavour. Sometimes the mixture included oranges. Surprisingly, milk was
also an ingredient in many of the early recipes. These lemonades and
ice waters were considered more refreshing than the fortified alcoholic
beverages of the day, such as port.

OUR MODERN EQUIVALENT

6 lemons

2 cups (500 mL) granulated sugar

8 cups (2 L) cold water

Wash the lemons thoroughly in warm, soapy water. Rinse well and let dry. Pare strips of the outer rind from 3 of the lemons and place the strips in a large pitcher. Squeeze the juice from all 6 lemons, add to the rinds with the sugar and stir well. Stir in the water. Refrigerate until cold, about 2 hours, or up to 1 day.

To serve, strain into glasses.

Makes 10 to 12 servings.

❀   ❀   ❀   ❀

TIP Serve over ice, with a slice of lemon as a garnish in each glass.

Fresh Strawberry Water

TAKE one pottle of strawberries and pick the stalks from them; pass them through a sieve with your wooden spoon; and put in two large spoonfuls of powdered sugar; squeeze one lemon, and let the rest be water; make it palatable, pass it through a sieve and it is fit for use.

HISTORIC RECIPE EXCERPTED FROM

*The Complete Confectioner;
or The Whole Art of Confectionery*
(Frederick Nutt, 1789)

~ FRESH STRAWBERRY WATER ~

A perfectly lovely and refreshing drink to enjoy with fresh strawberries.
You can also use individually quick-frozen berries when fresh
local berries are out of season.

HISTORICAL BACKGROUND

A "pottle" is a small cone-shaped basket used to hold strawberries and other soft fruit. The wild strawberries gathered around York were as flavourful as cultivated berries from the Old World. Elizabeth Simcoe wrote in her diary on June 27, 1792, "An Irish Captain gave us a basket of wild strawberries which were as large and well flavoured as the best scarlet strawberries in gardens in England."

OUR MODERN EQUIVALENT

4 cups (1 L) strawberries

⅓ cup (80 mL) superfine granulated sugar

Juice of 1 lemon

2 cups (500 mL) cold water

Rinse and hull the berries. Either whirl them in a food processor until you have a smooth purée, or crush them with a potato masher. Press the purée through a sieve into a large bowl.

Add the sugar and lemon juice and then the water, and stir until the sugar dissolves. Cover and refrigerate until cold, about 2 hours.

Makes 5 to 6 servings.

❁　❁　❁　❁

TIP Serve over ice, with a whole berry as a garnish.

HOW TO MEASURE INGREDIENTS FOR THE MODERN EQUIVALENTS

Use standard measuring spoons for small amounts of liquid or dry ingredients. Measures should be level.

For large amounts of liquid ingredients, use a glass measuring cup with a spout. Set the cup on a flat surface, and while looking at the cup from the side, fill the cup to the desired amount.

For larger amounts of dry ingredients, use a nesting set of dry measuring cups, usually metal or plastic. For all-purpose flour and granulated sugar, spoon the flour or sugar into the desired-size cup. Level off with a straight-sided knife. Avoid shaking the cup to level dry ingredients. For other ingredients such as currants, simply fill to the brim, but do not pack.

ADDITIONAL READING

Bridge, Tom and English, Colin Cooper. *Dr. William Kitchener Regency Eccentric Author of the Cook's Oracle.* East Sussex: Southover Press, 1992.

Davidson, Alan. *The Oxford Companion to Food.* Oxford: Oxford University Press, 1999.

Day, Ivan. *Cooking in Europe 1650–1850.* West Port: Greenwood Press, 2009.

———. *Ice Cream.* United Kingdom: Shire Publications Ltd., 2011.

Feltoe, Richard. *Redcoated Ploughboys The Volunteer Battalion of Incorporated Militia of Upper Canada, 1813–1815.* Toronto: Dundurn Press, 2012.

Firth, Edith G. *The Town of York 1793–1815.* Toronto: University of Toronto Press, 1962.

Fitzgibbon, Theodora. *The Food of the Western World.* New York: Quadrangle/New York Times Books, 1976.

Grigson, Jane. *English Food.* United Kingdom: Penguin Books, 1998.

Hess, Karen. *Martha Washington's Booke of Cookery.* New York: Columbia University Press, 1981.

Paston-Williams, Sara. *The Art of Dining: A History of Cooking and Eating.* London: National Trust, 1993.

Quale, Eric. *Old Cook Books: An Illustrated History.* New York: Brandywine Press, E.P. Dutton, 1978.

Robertson, Ross J. *The Diary of Mrs. John Graves Simcoe.* Toronto: Prospero Books, 2001.

Visser, Margaret. *The Rituals of Dinner.* New York: Penguin Books, 1991.

Willan, Anne. *Great Cooks and Their Recipes, from Taillevant to Escoffier.* United Kingdom: McCraw-Hill Book Company, 1977.

White, Florence. *Good Things in England.* United Kingdom: Futura Publications Ltd., 1974.

Anonymous. *Adam's Luxury, and Eve's Cookery; Or, The Kitchen-Garden Display'd. . . To Which is Added the Physical Virtues of Every Herb and Root.* London: R. Dodsley, 1744; facsimile edition London: Prospect Books, 1983.

The first third of this book instructs us on how to grow fruits and vegetables, the second section is a collection of recipes and the last section is dedicated to medicinal uses of plants.

Anonymous. *The Cook Not Mad; Or, Rational Cookery.* Kingston, Upper Canada: James MacFarlane, 1831; reprinted by The Cherry Tree Press, 1982.

The Cook Not Mad, although credited with the status of being the first cookery book published in Canada, was not Canadian written. It was a copy of an American book with the same title published in 1830 in Watertown, New York.

Anonymous. *The Lady's Companion.* London: printed for J. Hodges on London Bridge and R. Baldwin, 6th edition, Volume 2, 1753.

Cleland, Elizabeth. *A New and Easy Method of Cookery.* Edinburgh: facsimile of the 1755 edition; Berwick upon Tweed: Paxton Trust; Totnes: Prospect Books, 2005. With an introduction by Peter Brears.

Elizabeth Cleland ran a cooking school in Edinburgh and wrote this cookbook for her students.

Dods, Margaret. *The Cook and Housewife's Manual.* Edinburgh: Oliver
and Boyd; London: Simpkin and Marshall, 5th edition, 1833.
Mistress Margaret Dods was the pseudonym of Christine Isabel
Johnstone (1781–1857). She adopted the name from the innkeeper
in Sir Walter Scott's novel *St. Ronan's Well* (1824). Mrs. Johnstone
was a fine Scots cook, and her affinity for fine French cooking is
obvious throughout her recipes.

Eales, Mary. *The Compleat Confectioner.* London: J. Brindley, 1718.
Mary Eales claimed to have been the confectioner to Queen Anne.

Farley, John. *The London Art of Cookery.* London: John Barker, 9th
edition, 1800.
John Farley was the principal cook at the popular middle-class
London Tavern.

Glasse, Hannah. *The Art of Cookery Made Plain and Easy.* London:
facsimile of the 1747 edition; London: reprinted with glossary and
index by Prospect Books, 1983.

———. *The Art of Cookery Made Plain and Easy.* London: facsimile
of the 1796 edition; Hamden, Connecticut: Archon Books, 1971.
With an introduction by Fanny Craddock.

———. *The Compleat Confectioner: or The Whole Art of Confectionary
Made Plain and Easy.* London: I. Pottinger and J. Williams, 1760.
Hannah Glasse was an entrepreneur: she was a dressmaker and

milliner, and she authored two cookery books and a book for servants. Her cooking style was plain and hearty, unlike that of many of her contemporaries who were influenced by the grander French cuisine. *The Art of Cookery Made Plain and Easy* (1747) was her first book. Despite the success of her books, she landed in bankruptcy court.

Kitchener, Dr. William. *The Cook's Oracle,* New York: J & J Harper, 1830. Dr. Kitchener first published his bestselling cookbook *The Cook's Oracle* in London in 1817. He had a degree in medicine from Glasgow University but was not allowed to practise medicine in London. He is well known for his eccentricity as a "gourmand" and for giving elaborate dinner parties at his residence at 43 Warren Street, Fitzroy Square, London.

Markham, Gervais. *The English Housewife, Containing the Inward and Outward virtues Which Ought to Be in a Complete Woman.* London: 1615; Ed. Michael R. Best; Canada: McGill-Queen's University Press, 1986.

Massialot, F. *New Instructions for Confectioners in the Court and Country Cook.* London, n.p., 1702.

Mason, Charlotte. *The Lady's Assistant.* London: facsimile of 1787 edition; Bedford, Massachusetts: Applewood Books, 2009. Charlotte Mason is credited with the first written recipe for making sandwiches.

Moxon, Elizabeth. *English Housewifry. Exemplified In above Four Hundred and Fifty Receipts, Giving Directions in most Parts of Cookery.* Leedes: Griffith Wright, 1764.

Nutt, Frederick. *The Complete Confectioner; or The Whole Art of Confectionary.* London: printed for author; sold by J. Mathews, 1789.

Frederick Nutt was an apprentice of an Italian confectioner named Domenico Negri who had a shop in Berkeley Square, London, which was called The Pot and Pineapple.

Raffald, Elizabeth. *The Experienced English Housekeeper.* Manchester: facsimile of 1769 edition; East Sussex: Southover Press, 1997. With an introduction by Roy Shipperbottom.

Mrs. Raffald was a housekeeper for Lady Elizabeth Warburton in Cheshire. She moved to Manchester with her husband, John, and had a family with as many as 16 children. There she ran a confectioner's shop, opened a registry for servants and ran the Bull's Head Inn.

Roberts, Robert. *The House Servant's Directory.* Boston: Monroe and Francis, n.d.; New York: Charles F. Francis, 1827.

Robert Roberts wrote *The House Servant's Directory* while butler to Christopher and Rebecca Gore of Waltham, Massachusetts. It went into a second edition in 1828. He felt that servants were deficient in the necessary skills, deportment and attitude for employment in a gentleman's family, so wrote this directory as a manual.

Rundell, Maria Eliza. *A New System of Domestic Cookery, Formed Upon the Principles of Economy.* London: J. Murray, Fleet Street and J. Harding, St. James's Street, 1806.

Maria Rundell (1745–1828) intended her cookery book to be "for the conduct of the families of the authoress's own daughters" rather than for "the professed cooks," so she emphasized middle-class economy. The first edition (1806) was published anonymously, but the numerous reprints credited Mrs. Rundell as author.

Salmon, William. *The Family Dictionary; Or, Household Companion.* London: H. Rhodes, 1710. Dr. Salmon was an eccentric practising medical doctor, who wrote *The Family Dictionary* in 1696 as a practical guide to domestic medicine.

Smith, Eliza. *The Compleat Housewife.* London: printed for J. Pemberton at the Golden Buck, 1727.

The first edition of *The Compleat Housewife* was published in 1727 and other editions followed until 1773. Eliza Smith's cookbook was popular in America and an edited version was printed in the 1750s in Williamsburg, Virginia, by William Parks.

Verral, William. *A Complete System of Cookery*. London: printed for the author and sold by him; also sold by Edward Verral, bookseller in Lewes, and John Rivington, 1759.
William Verral learned his culinary skills from his father, Dick, the master of the White Hart Inn in Lewes, and Mssr. St. Clouet, the master cook for the Duke of Newcastle. Verral succeeded his father as master of the White Hart Inn.

GENERAL INDEX

INDEX OF RECIPES BY ORIGINAL
AUTHOR AND COOKBOOK

ABOUT THE EDITORS

Elizabeth Baird has been shaping Canada's culinary landscape for more than three decades. The author and co-author of many cookbooks, she had a long-running weekly column, "The Canadian Cookbook," in the *Toronto Star,* and was the food editor for *Canadian Living magazine* for 20 years. Elizabeth now writes the weekly column "Baird's Bites" for the *Toronto Sun* and is a volunteer historic cook at Fort York.

Bridget Wranich is a culinary historian and an expert on late 18th- and 19th-century cooking in Upper Canada. She has worked in museum education for over 25 years and is the programme officer at Fort York, where she develops and leads programs for the over 40,000 students and visitors to the site. She leads the Volunteer Historic Cooks in researching, testing and preparing recipes for the Foodways Programme. Bridget is a co-founder of the Culinary Historians of Canada.

The Volunteer Historic Cooks at Fort York are dedicated food history enthusiasts who meet weekly at the Fort to research, test and prepare recipes for cooking classes, demonstrations, ceremonies and special occasions such as Queen Charlotte's Ball. They have developed a line of historical baked goods and preserves for sale in the Fort's canteen. The volunteers regularly animate the historic kitchen, cooking from 18th and 19th-century recipes and bringing the rich culinary heritage of Canada to life, to the delight of visitors, who always enjoy the samples.